PURDUE UNIVERSITY NORTH CENTRAL

THE HISTORY OF A REGIONAL CAMPUS

EDITED BY

Joseph Coates & James S. Pula

Dedicated to the Generations of Students, Faculty, Staff, and Community Supporters Who Made PNC Possible

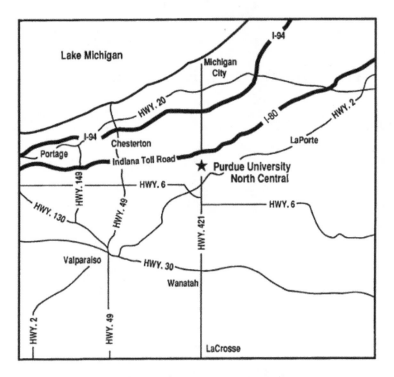

© Academic Consulting, 2019

ISBN 978-0-941504-02-7

CONTENTS

Acknowledgements

The editors are indebted to Tammy Guerrero and the Purdue University Northwest Archives for the use of its material and permission to use photographs from its collections; to Emily Reth, Director of the Barker Mansion & Civic Center, for permission to use photographs from the Barker Mansion archives; to the Board of Trustees of Purdue University for the use if its minutes and data collections; to the late K.R. Johnson, director of the PNC library, for his assiduous collection of PNC materials; and to the members of the Westville Study Committee whose work provided important data and information.

Appreciation is also due to the following individuals who provided assistance and material that aided the successful completion of this project: David Feikes, Julie Feikes, Deborah M. Kohler, Karen Prescott, Kim Scipes, Jeff Shires, Anthony Sindone, Diane Spoljoric, Anastasia Trekles, Donna Whitten, and Jennifer Williams.

INTRODUCTION: HOW IT ALL BEGAN

Joseph Coates

When I started as the University Archivist at Purdue University Calumet (PUC), we had an archive, albeit not in the best condition, but we had one. Although we had hundreds of collections in process, we had one go-to item. When people would ask a question about a date, an event, fun fact or for a decent photo, the first source would be Lance Trusty's book, *Purdue University Calumet: The First Fifty Years*.[1] This was a comprehensive history of the university written by a long time faculty member to celebrate this milestone. It was the easiest item to access for anyone at the university. Fast forward to 2016 to the unification of the Purdue Calumet and Purdue North Central (PNC) campuses and we began to form the archives in Westville. I started asking around and looking for a similar item, something that told the basic history of the institution. Well, that resource just did not exist.

The archives in Westville started by receiving donations of papers from all over campus. After cleaning out the chancellor's office, marketing, various closets and storerooms, we started to find the materials we needed to trace the history of the institution. All the course catalogs, self-studies, press releases, and a fantastic collection of scrapbooks of newspaper clippings gave us much of the needed information to begin assembling the history of the university.

As we were collecting, weeding, organizing, and working on finding aids for the PNC historic archive, it became evident that the history of PNC needed an easy-to-use-resource, something everyone could turn to for a general history of the institution. We needed a book, much like the PUC book, as a go-to item for people looking for the history of PNC. Writing that history was going to be a daunting task, especially for someone who does not have the opportunity to spend a lot of time writing and conducting research. In just the short time I had after starting the archives, I found quite a few documents written by former administrators of PNC describing what first Purdue Barker Center, then Purdue North Central was, or was not, depending on the memo.

One of the first documents I found was an institutional self-study written by Robert Schwarz that contained a brief history of the Purdue system.[2] He covered it in bullet points that included numerous facts. This is that history in a narrative form. In 1865, the Indiana General

Purdue University designated Ralph E. Waterhouse to be the first extension program representative for the north-western region of the state. (PNW Archives)

Vermont Senator Justin Morrill, a founder of the Republican Party, was responsible for the Morrill Land Grant Act, the basis for establishing Purdue University. (Library of Congress)

Assembly voted to take advantage of the Morrill Land-Grant Colleges Act of 1862 and began plans to establish an institution with a focus on agriculture and engineering. The result was the founding of Purdue University in 1869. In 1935, University officials resolved to bring education to the LaPorte area rather than have students travel to the Purdue West Lafayette campus. This was the beginning of a remarkable advancement in college extension centers. Purdue established about a hundred centers throughout Indiana to train skilled workers for defense industries. University officials selected Ralph E. Waterhouse to be the district representative of the extension program for LaPorte, Michigan City, and the entire Northwest Indiana region including Hammond, Gary, and East Chicago.

In September of 1946, the university launched an extension program that was the forerunner of the present regional campuses. As veterans returned to the university under the G.I. Bill, first-year classes were taught at some of these sites to alleviate the demand for campus

Purdue began offering extension classes at Central Junior High School in LaPorte in September 1946. This was the beginning of a presence in LaPorte County that would eventually lead to the development of Purdue University North Central and a permanent campus in Westville. (PNW Archives)

space. The Hammond, East Chicago, and Gary extension centers became the Purdue University Calumet Campus (PUC) while the LaPorte and Michigan City centers were transformed into the Purdue North Central (PNC) campus. The entire extension center program began in the public-school buildings of the various cities. In LaPorte, classes were conducted at the former Central Junior High School on 412 Harrison St. and at the Old LaPorte High School at 1000 Harrison Street.

The extension center program offered the full first-year of freshman engineering as well as a two-year technical institute. The LaPorte and Michigan City centers were considered a joint operation staffed with the same faculty, with time allotted for commuting, teaching, meetings, and counseling.

The original faculty were Leo Applegarth, Edgar Gracie, Walter Hansen, Harold Herod, Thomas Jacobson, Frederick Lisarelli, Howard Murdock, Thomas Nunn, Thomas Reynolds, Joseph Thalman, and Louis Ward. During the first two years of the PNC extension program, and largely because of the returning GIs, the LaPorte-Michigan City opera-

Completed under the direction of the noted Chicago architect Frederick Perkins in 1905, classes opened at the "Purdue-Barker Memorial Center" in the fall of 1949. (PNW Archives)

tion began with a total of 125 freshman and 30 technical institute students. The extensions' second year, however, witnessed an unfortunate decline to 50 freshmen in LaPorte and 25 in Michigan City. The fall of 1948 saw a further student enrollment loss in both centers with a consequent reduction of faculty members. At this time the university administration began considering eliminating the extension operation completely. Largely through the efforts of Waterhouse, the Northwest Indiana district representative, Purdue accepted the donation of Michigan City's Barker Mansion from its owner Catherine Barker Hickox. With the property, Purdue continued the operation, moving out of both school systems and into the Barker Mansion that became known as the "Purdue-Barker Memorial Center." The faculty had been reduced to three members Frederick R. Lisarelli, Howard Murdock and Thomas R. Nunn due to the downturn in enrollment, and if it were not for the Barker donation PNC would probably have never existed.

The first classes opened at the "Purdue-Barker Memorial Center" in the fall of 1949 with some very extraordinary facilities greeting the pioneering students. Former servants' quarters became faculty offices, the mansion's ten bathrooms were converted into science laboratories, a large sitting room served as a faculty lounge, while the spacious ball-room proved an excellent facility for drafting classes. Mrs. Barker's bedroom became a classroom, while the huge living room functioned as a student lounge, complete with rich wall-to-wall carpeting and a $3,000 piano.

In addition to offering freshman-sophomore courses and the School of Technology's two-year associate degree program, graduate courses were included for teachers pursuing master's degrees. Nevertheless, enrollment remained low, varying from about 25 to 40 per year through 1956. Waterhouse named Robert F. Schwarz his assistant, with Schwarz being designated as director of the Barker Center when Water-house died in June of 1954.

Although this was a very truncated account of the origin of PNC, it really did not focus on the people or events that took place. Since my association with Purdue Calumet, Purdue North Central, and now Purdue Northwest, we have always emphasized experiential learning. This gave me an idea. What if we let our students write the book? We could have our history students conduct the research, write the chapters, and tell the story of our university. I could not think of a better project than having our students use the skills they learn here and apply them to record our history. In the archive field, we spend a lot of time talking about putting archives in the classroom, this seems like the best use I can think of to create a real, tangible experience.

While developing this idea, Prof. James Pula was embarking on a similar project on the Westville Campus. Together, we decided to move forward with a joint effort using our respective skills and experience to best advantage. Fortunately, we were quickly able to assemble an interested and talented group of authors who all had personal experience as students at PNC. Josh Birky and Edward M. Rosary, both graduates of PNC, were completing work on their graduate degrees with its descendant, Purdue University Northwest. Aaron McWaters and Joshua Koepke were advanced undergraduate students on the Westville campus, both having already achieved membership in the Phi Alpha Theta National History Honorary. Jackie Perkins, the Heritage Interpreter at the Barker Mansion, was a graduate of PNC.

We hope this book is helpful to the PNC community. It is an interesting story to tell that brings back fond memories to many people. It is an important part of the history of the Barker family, Purdue University, LaPorte County, Porter County, Starke County, Westville and all of the students, faculty, and staff who made it a part of their own lives.

[1] Lance Trusty, *Purdue University Calumet: The First Fifty Years* (Hammond, IN: Purdue University Calumet, 1996).

[2] The following brief narrative of the beginning of PNC is taken from Robert Schwarz, "First Ten Years of P.N.C. History," PNW Archives. All references to the PNW Archives hereafter refer to the Westville Campus archives unless otherwise indicated.

THE BARKER YEARS: 1946-1967

Josh Birky

Deeply ingrained in the American character is the belief that education is the great equalizer, the key that unlocks the potential for achievement of life's ambitions. Founded in 1869 as Indiana's public land grant institution, the mission of Purdue University has always been to address the needs of the citizens of the state through education. The beginnings of Purdue University North Central grew out of this mission. The Servicemen's Readjustment Act of 1944, better known as the "GI Bill," led to a post-war boom in demand for higher education. At Purdue, enrollment doubled from 5,628 in the fall of 1945 to 11,462 a year later. In response, the university followed its land grant mission, opening over forty extension centers throughout the state to bring education to citizens where they resided.[1]

The mid-twentieth century presented many employment opportunities to the people of LaPorte County and surrounding areas. With industry booming and veterans soon returning from war, a new form of training became necessary. Purdue began offering classes at Central Junior High School in LaPorte and Elston High School in Michigan City in September 1946 with the sites administered jointly by Ralph E. Waterhouse. The first year drew 125 students in the freshman program, with 30 in the two-year technical institute – all males. Although enrollment dropped the next two years, Waterhouse's persistent arguments about the potential of the area led Purdue officials to seek a more permanent centralized facility. It was at this point that the future of what would become Purdue University North Central became entwined with the prominent Barker family of Michigan City.[2]

The author would like to thank Profs. James Pula, Joseph Coates, Michael Lynn, and Michael Connolly, each of who took time to meet with him and offer assistance throughout his college career.

John Barker, Sr., arrived in Michigan City in 1836. He became a very successful merchant, grain broker, and pioneer railroad entrepreneur. (Barker Mansion)

John H. Barker, Jr., took over the family business, becoming president of the company in 1883. (Barker Mansion)

In 1836, John Barker, Sr., emigrated from Andover, Massachusetts to Michigan City, Indiana, looking for work. He quickly became a successful businessman as a general merchant and grain broker. In 1855, the railroad industry was quickly expanding and Barker bought into a freight car manufacturing plant. Three years later, the company changed its name to the Haskell and Barker Car Company. Barker married in 1841 and sired five children, of which three survived including his son, John H. Barker. The Civil War caused the company to prosper and shortly after, in 1869, Barker Sr. retired. John H. took over for his father and became president of the company in 1883.[3]

John H. was a successful businessman before working for the Car Works. His skill manifested itself when the business grew to a capacity of 15,000 freight cars a year by 1910. This translated into great wealth for the Barker family, between fifty and sixty million dollars. John H. Barker married twice, losing his first wife and all three children to illnesses. He married his second wife, Katherine, in 1893 and had a daughter named Catherine three years later. Their magnificent home, later to house the college, was completed in 1905. It contained thirty-eight rooms, seven fireplaces, ten bathrooms, and hand crafted marble and wood, emitting elegance throughout. It also had a vacuum system, an early intercom system, and ducts to run cool air throughout the home. Both John H. and Katherine Barker died in 1910, leaving Catherine a fourteen-year-old orphan. Catherine was serious about using her money wisely, but was also inclined toward philanthropy. She created the Barker Annuity Fund in 1924 to care for the workers of Barker and Haskell after the company was sold to Pullman. In 1934 she founded the Barker Welfare Foundation to support non-profit organizations in Michigan City.[4]

In 1935, Purdue University began the process of creating extension centers throughout the state of Indiana to better serve students where they were located, rather than requiring them to journey to West Lafayette. The cities of LaPorte and Michigan City, working with Purdue, created a survey of area businesses and employees before the war, during the war, and their projected estimate after the war to determine if the two areas were suitable for extension centers. The 1944 survey teamed with each town's chambers of commerce to cover all the industries and other businesses in the area. Their survey used the 1940 census to support its claims. In 1940, LaPorte consisted of 19,180 citizens and Michigan City had a population of 26,476. LaPorte looked at the fourteen industrial businesses in the town, excluding the Kingsbury Ordinance plant, a business that provided Allied troops with ammunition. The 14 businesses surveyed employed 87 percent of the total employment. Table 1 shows the employment records for LaPorte, including the estimates for after the war.[5]

TABLE 1 — LAPORTE EMPLOYMENT DATA

	Pre-war 1941		August 1944		Est. Post-war	
	Men	Women	Men	Women	Men	Women
Industrial Concerns	3,677	845	4,540	1,926	5,433	1,081
Other Employers	2,342	940	2,040	1,110	2,752	1,133
Total	6,019	1,785	6,580	3,036	8,185	2,214

Ten of the fourteen businesses in the survey were metal manufac-turers. "The vocational technical training survey conducted by the U.S. Office of Education indicate that eight technicians should be employed in metal products manufacturing companies for each engineer."[6] In the fourteen companies surveyed, there were 545 jobs that needed technical training and 81 engineering graduates. The 545 to 81 led to a ratio of 6.72 technicians per engineer. Table 2 shows the number of technicians that needed to be trained in LaPorte in each field of study the Purdue Technical Institutes offered.

TABLE 2 — NEED FOR TECHNICIANS IN LAPORTE

Field of Study	Number of Jobs	Number Required Per Year Based on 35-Year Work Life
Technical Chemistry	15	.43
Industrial Design, Layout, Drafting	43	1.23
Technical Electricity	30	.86
Mechanical Principles and Practices	156	4.45
Industrial Metallurgy	3	.08
Production Technique, Supervision & Management	298	8.5
Total	545	15.6

TABLE 3 — NEED FOR TECHNICIANS IN MICHIGAN CITY

Field of Study	Number of Jobs	Number Required Per Year Based on 35-Year Work Life
Technical Chemistry	4	.11
Industrial Deign, Layout, Drafting	79	2.26
Technical Electricity	86	2.46
Mechanical Principles and Practices	58	1.67
Industrial Metallurgy	21	.60
Production Technique, Supervision & Management	471	13.46
Total	719	20.6

Michigan City had similar results. Eighteen industries employed 4,658, with estimates that employment in these industries would reach 5,990, surpassing the pre-war employment of 5,795. Thirteen of the eighteen companies manufactured metal. Like LaPorte, Michigan City recorded the number of technicians to engineers with 719 technicians needed for 87 engineers, a ratio of 8.27.[7] Table 3 shows the number of technicians that needed to be trained in Michigan City in each field of study offered by the Purdue Technical Institutes.

The survey ended with estimates of technical course completion and employment statistics, concluding that with a ten percent completion figure, the 160 enrollees at LaPorte and 210 in Michigan City would have no problem being incorporated into the workforce.[8]

Purdue officials named Ralph Waterhouse the district representative for the Northwest Indiana extension centers consisting of Hammond, Gary, East Chicago, Michigan City, and LaPorte. Two other extension centers were established in Fort Wayne and Indianapolis.[9] Classes began in the fall of 1946 in Michigan City and LaPorte ranging from varying technical classes to the freshman year engineering classes normally taught in West Lafayette. Each town's high school accommodated the extension centers, with classes held in the evenings.[10]

While classes were being held in the high schools of both LaPorte and Michigan City, Purdue officials began to plan for expansion. In March of 1946, Charles W. Beese and Harry C. Short met with the superintendents of Michigan City and LaPorte high schools. Before their meeting, the two men put together a background for the meeting where they planned on introducing the idea of using the Barker Mansion in Michigan City as a Technical Institute. By September 1946, the expansion center in Michigan City had 85 enrollees. These students attended part time, in the evenings, but the need for something full time, during the day became apparent. The Michigan City center began shipping twenty-one students to Hammond for full time study. With the returning veterans, and general interest in taking classes, the two men worried that the school would soon outgrow its facilities. "It appears likely for the next three years the influx of students will be greater than our physical plant can in any place begin to care for."[11]

Beese and Short believed based on the findings of the survey the year prior, that Michigan City and LaPorte industries had the ability to hire 50 technicians a year because of the recent growth within the industries. To fill that requirement, the men wrote that 125-150 students needed to enroll in entry level classes each year. The men's predictions of growth led to the need for a building, a centralized location that would accommodate program increases. Without ever seeing the inside of the building, the men decided the Barker Mansion in Michigan City would be the perfect location. Using only the blueprints, the men set up a fictitious school including classrooms, labs, offices, and a library. They spoke highly of the facility, and the benefits of having local businesses including Pullman-Standard and NIPSCO around to help shape the curriculum and offer graduates future positions. The cost of remodeling fell between $30,000 and $40,00. To recover the investment, the building needed to be used more than five years.[12]

At the same time Beese and Short were meeting with the superintendents of the high schools, one of Michigan City's most famous citizens, Carter H. Manny, corresponded with Catherine (Barker) Hickox, the heiress to the Barker fortune and owner of the Barker Mansion. Manny, a famous architect who studied under Frank Lloyd Wright, became interested in Purdue, specifically with the extension programs because of his experience as an industrial administrator. In his 1946 correspondence with Hickox, Manny praised the extension centers' programs, using Dwyer Products Corporation as an example. Dwyer employed a "top flight graduate engineer." "Such a plant employing two or three hundred people would not require more than one man of this qualification. However, there were places for a dozen men who might have training in the use of tools, reading of blueprints, chemistry, electricity, etc., without the other features of a college education."[13] Manny's letter was an encouragement to Hickox to donate the mansion to the University for the Technical Institute. His letter stressed the importance of the school to the area and how beneficial the building would be to the university. He insisted the house would be maintained as if it were still being used by the Barker family, something the city did not intend on initially doing when the building was first offered up. He wanted Catherine to know that donating the building to the school would make a lasting imprint not only on the school but also the town.

Manny suggested that if she named the building the Barker Center after her late father, Catherine could keep the Barker name alive for ages to come.

Veterans entered universities in astounding numbers due to the G.I. Bill which allowed them to buy homes, attend school, or get technical training. Nationally, 2,232,000 World War II veterans attended school assisted by the Bill. The entire program cost the government 5.5 billion dollars.[14] The amount of time for benefit allotments ranged from one to four years, based on time served and age of the recipient. Most veterans served more than three years, allowing for the maximum benefit of $500 in tuition per year and a $65 or $90 cash allowance per month depending on whether or not the veteran was married. To be eligible, the veteran needed to serve at least ninety days and have a honorable discharge. "Those who served on active duty between September 1940 and July 1947 were eligible, with the stipulation that they commenced schooling by July 1951."[15] The goal of the Bill, supported by the American Legion, was to take care of the people who sacrificed for the country better than the country did after World War I. While it was being debated in Congress, Legion National Commander Warren H. Artherton issued a warning. "Veterans 'will be a potent force for good or evil in the years to come. They can make our country or break it. They can restore our country or scrap it.... We do not want our sons and daughters selling apples on street corners.'"[16] The G.I. Bill succeeded in its objective, "with over a million veterans crowding on American campuses during the banner year of 1947-48."[17] The growth of the student body, as well as the counties surrounding the extension centers, led to an increased push for the creation of a legitimate technical institute.

In late 1946 as enrollment numbers were increasing and the need for something new became apparent, a meeting of the Association of Land Grant Colleges and Universities took place. Beese, an engineering professor from Purdue, read a paper entitled, "What is a Technical Institute?" According to him, "the technical institute is viewed as an activity of the Land Grant College closely allied to the professional engineering curricula."[18] Purdue was established as a land grant college in 1869 focusing on engineering, technology and agriculture. A technical institute extension in Northwest Indiana made sense to many professors and citizens of that region due to the immense amount of industry and growth in the area. Beese noted that supporters believed "the technical institute is an opportunity for them to do something different from the usual pattern of university activity. It brings them closer to industry and to the educational problems in a community. It performs a welcome service to its students, to the community, and to industry, and thereby gains a lot of friends with whom it is pleasant to work."[19] Beese's goal in giving this speech was to reestablish the extension centers as technical institutes. He promoted the classes and programs technical institutes offered. When high school students graduated, they generally had a handful of choices including college, military service, or joining the workforce. The problem that many encountered pertained to the need for some sort of technical training to do jobs like reading or drawing blueprints. The technical institute became the solution for people in this predicament. Beese considered the gap that many high school graduates fell into as a "blind spot." He wrote, "The technical institute attempts to fill the gap that is referred to above. The courses are terminal in character. Curricula are one or two years in length. The courses are practical and applied, rather than theoretical. They deal with immediate situations which are met at the job."[20] With Beese's description and the reality of the job market in LaPorte County, a technical institute fit perfectly within the community.

Another benefit of a technical institute occurred when it was yoked with a land grant university based on engineering. Beese argued four points as to why the benefits occurred. First, a technical institute used the established curriculum of the land grant university. Second, the curriculum created a level of prestige for the technical institute. Third, the reputation of the state school-backed technical institute led to better job placement because of knowledge of the state school. Fourth, the land grant university benefited from the contacts created by the technical institute.[21]

In 1947 an enrollment campaign took place from July to September at the LaPorte County Fair, in local newspapers, and with graduating seniors from LaPorte County and the surrounding areas. Some 1,442 potential high school graduates received "a technical institute pamphlet, a freshman program pamphlet, and a reply card."[22] Of those contacted,

Catherine Barker Hickox as she appeared in 1915. She made possible the consolidation of the Purdue extension sites in LaPorte and Porter Counties into a single building in Michigan City. (Barker Mansion)

379 requested interviews that included the following: "an introductory explanation of the extension program, the development of individual's educational interests, an explanation of the particular extension program best suited to those interests, and a discussion of the possibilities of utilizing the extension services available at LaPorte or Michigan City."[23] At the fair, 5,000 freshman pamphlets, 4,000 technical institute pamphlets, and 5,200 miscellaneous pamphlets and bulletins were distributed. During the six days of the fair, 636 people stopped and made personal contact while 128 requested meetings at the centers.[24]

The promotion that reached the most people was the newspaper campaign. The August 6, 1947, issue of the Starke County *Democrat* ran an article entitled "Technical Institute Training Offered at LaPorte and Michigan City." It covered all six of the fields of training offered at the centers, praised the system, and encouraged readers to explore the options.[25] Despite the efforts of the fair, the mailed information, and the ad campaigns in the newspapers, according to Professor Fred Lisarelli, the original 155 students (125 freshmen, 30 technical students) in 1946 dropped by fifty freshmen while the technical students remained the same in 1947.[26] In 1948, enrollment once again fell, so low in fact that Purdue nearly dissolved the centers.

Despite the enrollment drop, a massive change took place in these two years that benefited the school immensely. Talks to obtain the Barker Mansion became a reality. In the years prior, Catherine (Barker) Hickox had been looking for a beneficial way to use the home. Once

These students, their images reflected in the pristine table top, study on period antique chairs with an elaborate china closet to the left and rich tapestry window curtains in the background. (PNW Archives)

she nearly gave it to the city to use as a civic center, another time to a maritime school.[27] Neither occurred and the home stayed in the Barker family. For many months following the initial letter in 1946, Manny spoke with Hickox, encouraging her to believe in the technical institute's mission and to work with Purdue to create a permanent home. C. W. Beese, Director of the Technical Extension Division, assisted Manny by encouraging Purdue University President Fredrick Hovde about the project and convincing him to write to Hickox. Beese suggested the letter address not only the need for a permanent residence, but also that the sentimental memory of her family would stay intact within the house, something the prior inquiring organizations did not promise. He also urged Hovde to suggest that the school would continue the legacy of her father with innovation and industry.[28]

Some of the first women to enroll at PNC gather next to a huge window in a "lounge" at the Barker Center complete with imported furniture and wallpaper. Note the more formal attire that was considered proper then for attending university classes, as well as the saddle shoes and Purdue "Block P" sweater. (PNW Archives)

While the number of students in 1948 sagged to the point of nearly closing the extension centers, M. L. Knapp, the superintendent of Michigan City Schools, Beese, Hovde, and especially Ralph Waterhouse, finally came to an agreement with Hickox to donate the Barker Mansion to Purdue University.[29] The story of the donation made the cover of the Michigan City *News-Dispatch* on January 22, 1948. The article stated that Hickox donated the home with the precondition that the library, living room, and dining room be kept in period setting. She even agreed to have a maintenance crew hired to preserve the authenticity and cleanliness of the property. Because of the need to remove items from the house, and to undertake cleaning and educational renovation, the beginning of classes had to wait a year. According to the article,

Piles of books pose no problem for this large, ornately carved table that serves as a communal desk for a chemistry class led by Prof. Howard Murdock, one of the "Founding Four" faculty at PNC. Note that a folding chair has intruded on the scene amidst the original furnishings. (PNW Archives)

they would eventually feature "Technical and scientific training for both young and adult students in the industries of the area, training in some economics and agriculture, short courses, conferences and symposia for teachers and other professions are contemplated for the program to be carried out in the Barker Memorial center."[30] With the donation of the building, the Michigan City and LaPorte centers combined at this single location.

Though complete elimination of the extension centers was subverted by obtaining a building, the technical institute had a large obstacle to overcome: low enrollment. In fact, obtaining the Barker Center required Purdue to keep the school open. In a letter to Beese, Knapp expressed his concern. "Due to the fact that enrollment in the present term of the

Technical Institute here is quite disappointing, I am somewhat alarmed for the future of this project unless it receives some courageous and perhaps expensive treatment at the present time."[31] Knapp's reason for discouragement lay solely with the lack of students not supported by the G.I. Bill. Once veterans used their funding and went through the program, the number of students shrank drastically. He suggested that recruiting needed to be aimed more at the local high schools and within industries. The Technical Institute was not the only school suffering from low numbers. Knapp continued: "Presi-dent Wells of Indiana University last Sunday told the freshman class, numbering between 4,000 and 5,000, that their class is the first one since pre-war years that did not contain a con-

Robert F. Schwarz, a native of Missouri, received his A.B. in 1950 and M.S. in 1951, both from Indiana University. He arrived in Michigan City in October 1952 as assistant director of the Purdue Barker Memorial Center.

siderable number of G.I. students."[32] On top of a loss of students, Knapp indicated concern over the loss of faith in the institute by employers in the area. "I have seen a lessening of interest on the part of a few of our employers because of what they considered a poor quality of instruction in the earlier days of the Institute."[33]

Knapp believed the Barker Mansion as a centralized location would draw more interest, but would require determination and hard work to be successful in the long run. Knapp's concern was justified. With the loss of students came the loss of faculty. By the time the Barker Center opened for classes in the fall of 1949, the eleven original teachers dwindled down to three — Fredrick Lisarelli, Howard Murdock, and Thomas Nunn — who taught all of the classes. "Lisarelli taught all the freshman math and engineering drawing, Murdock all the chemistry and biology, Nunn all the English and social sciences. This was possible since there was only one section in any one course."[34]

With three faculty and only a few students, Purdue held its first classes at the Barker Center in September 1949 with some very extraordinary facilities greeting the pioneering students. Former servants' quarters became faculty offices, the mansion's ten bathrooms were converted into science laboratories, a large sitting room served as a faculty lounge, while the spacious ballroom proved an excellent facility for drafting classes. Mrs. Barker's bedroom became a classroom, while the huge living room functioned as a student lounge, complete with rich wall-to-wall carpeting and a $3,000 piano.

Over the next decade things began to turn around. The 1950s brought population growth to LaPorte and Porter counties, with corresponding business expansion. Porter County increased from 40,000 to 60,000 inhabitants between 1950 and 1960, while LaPorte County rose from 76,000 to 95,000.[35] In Michigan City, the Northern Indiana Public Service Company (NIPSCO) built a new power unit at their plant which created additional jobs. In the early half of the decade a co-op program began at the Barker Mansion campus. In a letter to A. R. Kessell, the plant manager at Joy Manufacturing, Ralph Waterhouse briefly described the program and its intent. "We have made a great effort to get high school (boys) graduates interested in the Purdue-Industry Co-op plan of work and study, to enable those wishing to qualify as engineering aides and technicians, to enroll in the program."[36] The schedule placed students in different industrial settings to give them job experience while they studied, an early example of what came to be called "experiential education" that continued into the years to come. G. W. Bergren, an associate professor in mechanical engineering, explained its three most important benefits. First, the student gained three semesters and two summers of both classroom and industrial work, which made both more meaningful. Second, the work helped pay for school. Third, because of the work experience, the student did not need training in the company and thus started at a higher paying position.[37]

In 1953, Purdue hired Robert F. Schwarz as the Barker Center Director. Schwarz served in this position for the balance of the school's stay at the Barker Mansion. When it eventually relocated, Schwarz became the first Dean and Director of Purdue University North Central, where he served until 1972. Schwarz played such an important role in the institution's livelihood that his nickname was "Mr. Purdue North Central."[38]

Schwarz inherited a program with about 100 students registered in 188 courses. Under his creative, energetic leadership, enrollment grew six-fold to more than 600 students by fall of 1966. Schwarz's enthusiasm, the expansion of enrollment and increasing local support led Purdue to purchase 155 acres of farmland along U.S. Route 421 just south of the Indiana Toll Road for a potential new campus. Dr. Charles H. Lawshe, dean of university extension, who made the formal announcement, noted that no state tax funds were involved in the purchase. A clearly pleased Schwarz added that "If we are able to develop the property acquired, it will place a major state university facility in touch with students from the tri-city areas of LaPorte, Valparaiso and Michigan City."[39]

An expanded curriculum included credit courses such as Psychology ($20), Industrial Organization and Production ($40) and Job Evaluation ($20) supplemented with a variety of non-credit courses like Blue Print Reading ($12), Landscape Gardening ($10) or Introduction to Radio Acting ($15). In 1957 television was used for the first time in regularly scheduled classes, with students watching a broadcast and then continuing with the balance of their class.

Students at the Barker Center identified closely with Boilermaker athletic teams. West Lafayette fostered this "one university" spirit with local appearances of musical groups, speeches by Purdue coaches and administrators and close ties between the Barker Mansion faculty and their counterparts in West Lafayette. In 1964, for example, a "Boilermaker Express" float won second prize of 134 units participating in the July 11 "Summer Festival Parade" in Michigan City. Its theme called upon prospective students to join the "Express to Success."[40]

The mid- to late-1950s changed the American landscape once again. The Cold War began in 1947, followed thereafter by the Space Race that began with the Soviet Union's launching of Sputnik in 1957. In an issue of *Technology and Culture*, Asif A. Siddiqi, noted that "The launch of Sputnik starkly accentuated the national identity and technol-

In this 1966 photograph, students at the Barker Center show their school spirit prior to Purdue's victory over the University of Southern California in the 1967 Rose Bowl. (PNW Archives)

ogy."[41] It also caused "A crisis of confidence [that] washed over most of American society, an anxiety that depended on an intrinsic equation between modern America and science and technology."[42] Politicians believed better education resulted in the Soviet launch of Sputnik, so money became available for higher education to combat the efforts of the Communists. During the years of the Cold War, America focused on technology and industry. This priority trickled down to the technical institute. While enrollment remained low during the early 1950s, by 1956, the Center had eighty-eight students, four of whom were studying full-time.

The national security interests of the Cold War era and the growth of both population and industry in LaPorte and Porter Counties, including the new Bethlehem Steel Mill, drew people into the workforce and

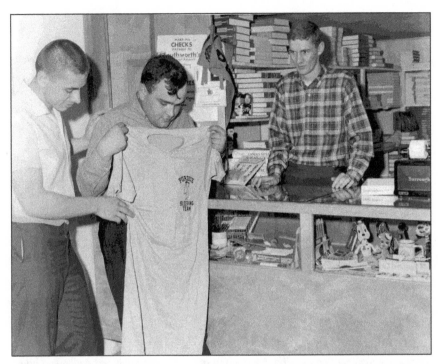

With limited space, the bookstore at the Barker Mansion was a small affair tucked under a staircase. Here a student admires a garment emblazoned with the logo of the "Purdue Sleeping Team." (PNW Archives)

subsequently to Purdue at the Barker Memorial Center. The two year training courses and the freshman engineering program drew in a steady flow of students, so much that by the late 1950s and early 1960s the Barker Center could no longer accommodate the number of students. The student body grew to a point that Purdue officials took notice. They realized something needed to be done, "and in 1962 the Ross-Ade Foundation a Purdue affiliate purchased 155 acres of rolling farm land just south of the intersection of U.S. 421 and the Indiana Toll Road as a future site for a North Central Campus."[43] The initial plan for the new facility was for a 1965 opening, but the groundbreaking did not occur until June of that year.[44]

In 1964, Schwarz, sensing the end of the Barker era, wrote a history of Purdue North Central. The school then enrolled 650 students, a great

Personal enrichment courses have been part of the Purdue adult and continuing edu-cation programs from its earliest days in the Barker Center. In this photograph, area women take part in a course in flower arranging taught by Mrs. Bernard Solberg. Around the table are (from left) Mrs. W. J. Scharnberg, Mrs. Harry Gloye, Mrs. R. Bernard Bowman, Mrs. Michael Joseph (standing), Mrs. David M. Crosthwaite and Mrs. John Feyling. (PNW Archives)

contrast to the dismal numbers a decade earlier. It employed "nine full time faculty, twenty part-time faculty, two administrators, two secretaries and two service staff."[45] The curriculum had also expanded. Schwarz's history explained that "The center offers the first year of studies in most of the Purdue curricula. In a few areas... secondary teaching, elementary education, and general liberal arts... students can obtain two full-years of work."[46] He also forecast that, with the eventual move, "Programs at the new site will be greatly broadened. It is hoped that two full years of most of the Purdue curricula will be available. Adult education programs will be expanded and there will be a greater emphasis on graduate work."[47]

Purdue North Central's inception occurred to educate local students to fill jobs in the industry of LaPorte County and the surrounding area. Through many trials, the fledgling Center persisted. When the North Central campus opened in 1967 over 1,200 students attended. Purdue North Central's cause of helping local students to better themselves at a reasonable cost would continue.

---

[1] James S. Pula, "Purdue North Central," unpublished manuscript, 2007.

[2] Ibid.

[3] Sarah Rogers, *Barker Mansion: Heritage with a Future* (Berrien Center, MI: Penrod/Hiawatha, 2000), 1-2.

[4] Ibid.

[5] "1945 Survey: Michigan City & LaPorte," 4, PNW Archives.

[6] Ibid., 5.

[7] Ibid.

[8] Ibid., 6.

[9] Robert Schwarz, "The History of Purdue North Central" (1964), PNW Archives.

[10] Letter, G. W. Beese and Harry C. Short, March 20, 1946, Meeting Correspondence, PNW Archives.

[11] Letter, Beese to Short, March 20, 1946.

[12] Ibid., 2-8.

[13] Letter, Carter H. Manny to Catherine Hickox, March 29, 1946. PNW Archives.

[14] Keith W. Olson, "The G.I. Bill and Higher Education: Success and Surprise," *American Quarterly*, Vol. 25, no. 5 (Dec. 1973), 596.

[15] John Bound and Sarah Turner, "Going to War and Going to College: Did World War II and the G.I. Bill Increase Educational Attainment for Returning Veterans?" *Journal of Labor Economics*, Vol. 20, no. 4 (Oct. 2002), 790.

[16] Olson, "The G.I. Bill and Higher Education," 598.

[17] Ibid., 602.

[18] C. W. Beese, "What is a Technical Institute?" Dec. 17, 1946, 2, PNW Archives.

[19] Ibid.

[20] Ibid., 3.

[21] Ibid., 4.

[22] "Report of Publicity Activities, July-September 1947," Purdue University Technical Extension Division, 2, PNW Archives.

[23] Ibid., 22.

[24] Ibid.

[25] "Technical Institute Training Offered at LaPorte and Michigan City," Starke County *Democrat*, Aug. 6, 1947.

[26] Fredrick Lisarelli, "The First Ten Years of P.N.C. History" (1976), 2, PNW Archives.

[27] Letter, M. L. Knapp to Harry Short, April 1, 1946, PNW Archives.

[28] Letter, C. W. Beese to Frederick Hovde, Mar. 13, 1947. PNW Archives.

[29] Lisarelli, "First Ten Years," 3.

[30] "Barker Homestead Given to Purdue University for Use as Class Center," *The News Dispatch*, Jan. 22, 1948.

[31] Letter, M. L. Knapp to C. W. Beese, Sept. 24, 1948. PNW Archives.

[32] Ibid.

[33] Ibid.

[34] Lisarelli, "First Ten Years," 3.

[35] See U.S. Census at https://www.census.gov/population/cencounts/in190090.txt

[36] Letter, Ralph Waterhouse to A. R. Kessell, June 9, 1952. PNW Archives.

[37] G. W. Bergman, "M.E. University-Industry Cooperative Education Program" (1956), 1, PNW Archives.

[38] "Purdue University North Central Silver Anniversary" (1992), 4, PNW Archives.

[39] Schwarz, "The History of Purdue North Central."

[40] Ibid.

[41] Asif A. Siddiqi, "Competing Technologies, National(ist) Narratives, and Universal Claims: Toward a Global History of Space Exploration," *Technology and Culture*, Vol. 51, no. 2 (Apr. 2010), 428.

[42] Ibid.

[43] "Purdue University North Central Silver Anniversary," 3.

[44] Ibid.

[45] Schwarz, "History of Purdue North Central," 2.

[46] Ibid.

[47] Ibid., 3.

"CAMPUS IN A CORNFIELD": 1962-1972

Aaron McWaters

Speaking to a group of Purdue alumni at Wellman's Restaurant in Valparaiso on April 20, 1967, Purdue President Frederick L. Hovde proudly stated that "Not since the state approved the site of the West Lafayette campus nearly 100 years ago has Indiana built a campus in a cornfield until construction began on the North Central Campus." Referencing Purdue University's origins as a land-grant college provided by the Morrill Act of 1862, Hovde contrasted the expected enrollment of 1,200 students for North Central's inaugural semester with the less than 40 students that first walked through the doors of Purdue West Lafayette in 1874, telling the gathered alumni that North Central "will have quite a head start" and stressing that the quality of both faculty and the new facilities would match that of the main campus. The development of Purdue North Central on 216 acres just north of Westville in LaPorte County was the culmination of years of planning on the part of both university and state officials, pointing to the importance of the new campus in the expansion of higher education in Northwest Indiana to keep up with regional economic growth and demand for educational opportunities and training that had pushed beyond the capabilities and capacity of the Barker Memorial Center in Michigan City.[1]

The establishment of a system of "satellite" campuses within the state marked the shift in Indiana's economy from one primarily built upon agriculture to an industrial economy, particularly in the northern counties of Lake, Porter, and LaPorte. The formation of regional campuses was "an outgrowth of the Engineering War Training Manpower Program of World War II in which Purdue University cooperated with the federal government to provide training for manpower which was essential to the war effort," while following the war the Trustees of Pur-

---

The author would like to thank his wife, Leslie, and his mother, Joyce, for helping him spend all the extra time in the archives.

due University worked with local communities to establish a number of extension centers that would be the precursors to the later regional campuses. These initial extension centers were funded through their local communities, along with enrollment fees and modest funding from West Lafayette. This changed in 1965, when the Indiana General Assembly first recognized the regional campuses in its appropriations, and again in 1969 when these campuses were given an operating appropriation that was distinct from the West Lafayette campus. This distinction in funding was instrumental in the "subsequent development of three of these regional campuses into degree granting institutions and the companion development of North Central's into a two-year institution."[2]

Initial plans to construct a new campus in Northwest Indiana to replace the Barker Memorial Center and centralize higher education classes throughout the region began to materialize in 1962 with Purdue officials conducting surveys in the LaPorte-Porter county region to determine a suitable location for expansion. In February, Indiana Senator John F. Shawley, who spent 18 combined years in the Indiana House of Representatives and Senate and was a driving force behind the North Central project as vice-chairman of the Post-High School Education Study Commission, announced that "a site of 100-155 acres about 10 to 12 miles south of Michigan City" was under consideration. Using the $3.5 million construction project of the Calumet Center as a model for future projects, Shawley believed that the North Central campus would not require any legislation or funding from the state, with the construction being covered by the university's building fund and student fees. This tract of land was confirmed as the site of future expansion by the announcement on May 21 that 155 acres adjacent to U.S. Highway 421, just north of Westville and south of the Indiana Toll Road had been purchased from the Long Beach Co. for $91,000 through the University affiliated non-profit Ross Ade Foundation. Later purchases of adjoining land pushed the campus to 216 acres, and eventually 305 acres.

The acquisition of land represented a significant step in the realization of a new Purdue facility being constructed in Northern Indiana, a long-time goal of both Shawley and University officials. Speaking on behalf of Purdue, Charles H. Lawshe, dean of University Extension, released a statement on the purchase, stating "We are very happy with the location of the property. Our studies indicate an increasing rate of growth of the industrial and residential area that is moving eastward from Lake County." It was hoped the site, roughly centralized between the cities of Valparaiso, LaPorte, and Michigan City, would appeal to students throughout the Porter-LaPorte region. The new North Central facility would provide students the opportunity to complete the first two years toward a four-year degree while offering both Associate Degree programs and technical training that continued in the tradition of the earlier post-war extension centers and relieving the pressure on the over -capacity Barker Memorial Center.[3]

Planning for the North Central campus occurred throughout 1963-64. Initial plans called for a single 70,000 square foot building at an estimated cost of $1.5 million for classrooms, with student service areas that could be converted to laboratory space as needed. Speaking at a dinner at the Westville Lions Club in April of 1963, Prof. Robert F. Schwarz, Director of the Purdue extension at the Barker Memorial Center, described the community as the ideal location for a new campus, a "geographic hub" between the major population centers in LaPorte and Porter counties. Citing the continued expansion of industry in the area and the corresponding influx of employment opportunities, Schwarz estimated that within 15 years the region's population would grow by 150,000 and was optimistic that by 1972 one out of two students in the area would enroll at the North Central campus rather than moving down -state to West Lafayette. Schwarz further emphasized the role of the campus as "primarily a technical university," although he left room for the future inclusion of an expanded curriculum that included four-year degrees in education and the liberal arts. In June, Dr. Lawshe announced a tentative construction schedule beginning in the early part of 1964 with the aim of completing the building in time to open for the school year beginning in September of 1965, a timeline that would be pushed back once construction began. The architects at Walter Scholer & Associates, out of Lafayette, were chosen to design the building.[4]

In May of 1964, the Board of Trustees in Lafayette, in order to "meet the demand for a substantial expansion of student enrollment capacity in north central Indiana," officially approved facilities "to be located on the branch campus of Purdue University in LaPorte County,

Indiana." Preliminary plans for the campus layout and sketches of the façade and floor plans for the initial building were displayed by R.T. Hamilton, Director of Physical Plant and Development Planning, and Dean Lawshe. The first building was "planned for ultimate use as a general science building," the ground floor composed of administrative offices and student services, with three floors of classrooms. Once finished, the facility would accommodate 500 full-time students. Financing of the $2.8 million project was done through the newly created Purdue Academic Facilities Foundation, which was "organized and operated exclusively" for "providing academic facilities for use of Purdue University" after it was decided that Ross-Ade, which held the title for the land, would "have difficulty in qualifying as an agency founded to provide educational facilities." Thus, the Trustees approved a plan whereby 40 percent of the total cost would be covered by the Federal Facilities Act with the remainder coming from a bank loan through the PAFF.[5]

The North Central campus was part of a larger push to expand higher education throughout Indiana in the early 1960s. In May of 1964, a "series of studies of long-range Indiana educational needs by the state's four publicly supported institutions of higher learning" were presented at the Indiana Conference of Higher Learning, where a number of recommendations were made to the coming 1965 Indiana General Assembly for approval. These studies, carried out by the Indiana Post High School Education Study Commission, corresponded with the Commission's finding reported to the 1963 General Assembly that "additional needs for public supported collegiate level education in Indiana be met by community campuses and extension centers of existing state institutions, and that to meet these needs the extension system be expanded and developed as appropriate." To this end, the 1964 Conference recommended the construction of four-year extension centers in the Calumet area, South Bend, Fort Wayne, and Indianapolis where an analysis by the four state schools projected the number of students to be "so large as to make four-year campuses essential" by 1973. Two-year institutions were likewise important for relieving the pressure on the major university campuses and the state's ability to keep up with projected growth, and university officials saw the Commission's report as a clear

"Let's build a campus!" From the left in this June 28, 1965, photo are John A. Garrettson of Michigan City; Charles, H. Lawshe, Dean of University Extension; Robert Schwarz, Dean and Director of Purdue Barker Center. (PNW Archives)

indication of the need for the North Central facility. Plans were expedited, with Schwarz indicating bids for construction could come before the new school year. In reference to the report, Schwarz stated the North Central campus would be of great benefit in meeting the goals of the Commission by "planning the first facilities at the 160-acre site to meet this immediate growth" in the need for educational facilities.[6]

While the construction bids did not come as early as Schwarz had hoped, July brought news reports that the Board of Trustees would likely begin reviewing bids at its meeting on October 21, along with the release of architectural renderings of the first building—named the Education Building—and a detailed description of the floor plan. Local newspapers printed an image of the proposed building along with the report, the first look that the people of the surrounding communities likely had of the new North Central Regional Campus. The sketch showed the outside of the 93,000 square-foot building that would house 15 classrooms, seven laboratories, two lecture rooms seating 100 students each, a library, and various student and administrative rooms. September brought provisional approval by the State Budget Committee of the University's plan to build the $2.8 million North Central campus with its own fees and earnings. Plans to take bids were delayed a few days prior to the October Board meeting, however, when it was learned that the federal funds the University was seeking under the Higher Education Facilities Act—accounting for nearly 40 percent of the total construction costs—would not be received until spring. It was still hoped that the campus would open in 1966.[7]

As winter thawed into the spring of 1965, the project was able to move forward, with bids at last being taken at Barker Memorial Center from April 21-23. At the May 5 meeting of the Board of Trustees, the bids of six companies were reviewed: M.A. Lombard & Son Co., E.H. Marhoefer Jr. Co., S.N. Nielsen Company, Schumacher Sons, Inc., Superior Construction Co., and Tonn & Blank, Inc. University Vice-President and Treasurer Lytle J. Freehafer reported that all bids were "substantially in excess" of the original estimate of $2.8 million, which was attributed to "the tremendous building program in the area resulting from the proposed port development and various steel company expansions." Tonn & Blank, Inc., of Michigan City, was ultimately chosen to build the new Education Building according to the designs of Walter Scholer and Associates, at a cost of slightly more than $2.7 million, bringing the total cost of the project to $3,427,000. Financing for the project was also firmed up; in addition to the September approval by the State Budget Agency for the use of fees and earnings and the federal grant under the Higher Education Facilities Act of $1,120,000, it was reported at the meeting that the Indiana National Bank of Indianapolis and the Lincoln National Life Insurance Company of Fort Wayne had "agreed to provide permanent financing for the project," although the change in the project's cost meant new approval had to be sought by state and federal officials.[8]

Construction underway to convert a cornfield into the Purdue North Central campus.
(PNW Archives)

Following the announcement in early June that the federal grant had been officially approved, a groundbreaking ceremony was at last scheduled for June 28. The event was attended by around 50 guests, mainly officials from the surrounding communities. Dean Schwarz presided. The front page of the LaPorte *Herald-Argus* of June 28 carried a photograph of Dean of University Extension Charles H. Lawshe turning over the first earth with a four-tined, chrome plated spading fork, each tine bearing a brass plate engraved with the name of one of the local communities: LaPorte, Michigan City, Valparaiso, and Westville. To the left and right of Lawshe are Russell Murtin, president of Westville's town board; Michigan City mayor Randall C. Miller; vice-president of the LaPorte Chamber of Commerce, William L. Taylor; and the mayor of Valparaiso, Thomas Will. The ceremony initiated the beginning of a 22-month construction schedule by Tonn and Blank; preliminary work had in fact already begun earlier in the week, and a final completion date was set for July of 1967. Schwarz expressed the satisfaction likely felt by all of the attending university and local officials: "After several years of planning and waiting, we will now see our dreams realized. The faculty and staff of the center are anxious to occupy the new facilities and start planning for the tremendous growth that we see ahead."[9]

THE NORTH CENTRAL REGIONAL CAMPUS

The first half-decade in the existence of the North Central Regional Campus was marked by rapid expansion. This was, in many respects, a continuation of the momentum that had been building up at the Barker Memorial Center, where nearly every semester had brought a new enrollment record. At last freed from the confines of the Michigan City mansion, the new campus experienced extraordinary growth at nearly every level, including not only the student population, but in degree programs, course offerings, and size, with the completion of the original building and the construction of an additional one. The groundwork was also laid for the eventual addition of four-year degree programs, beginning with Purdue North Central working toward receiving separate accreditation from the main campus in West Lafayette. Even as classes began for the first time in September of 1967, it was evident that university officials were already planning for the future. As dean Schwarz explained to a group of news reporters shortly after the semester began, "'Extension' is a dirty word to us now...we like to think of Purdue having five campuses—one of which just happens to be at Lafayette."[10]

After the fast pace of the years leading up to the groundbreaking in Westville in 1965, the intervening two years before the doors of North Central opened were relatively quiet, though it was not a period of inactivity. At the end of 1965 came the announcement of the addition of a two-year registered-nurse training curriculum that would begin at the Barker Memorial Center before transferring to the new campus. The program was innovative; through "concentrated and intensified schooling," it would enable students to take the test for state certification as registered nurses in two years, rather than the 3 years typically necessary. In early 1967 a new two-year computer technology course leading

The original "Campus in a Cornfield." Labeled the "Education Building," the first structure was later renamed Schwarz Hall in honor of the first campus administrator. (PNW
Archives)

to an Associate in Applied Science was announced, the first in the area.
Schwarz revealed that an IBM 360 Model 20 computer had been or-
dered, though would not be available for the first semester, which included initial courses for Unit Record Processing, Computer Program-
ming, Computer Statistics, and Computer Utilization, with more to be
added in the future.[11]

    In June of 1966 Lawshe promoted Schwarz to Dean and Director of
the program at the Barker Memorial Center, a position he would carry
over to Purdue North Central when it opened in 1967. In October PNC
enrolled its first two students, Kathleen Kienitz of Michigan City and
Cheryl Poteet of Laporte, both 16 years of age. The *Herald-Press* reported the completion of their registration as "a special distinction in
the history of Purdue University," describing the new students as

"scientific-minded young ladies," with Kienitz planning to major in mathematics and Poteet in zoology. It was not only regional students looking to attend classes at the new campus. In July of 1967 Japanese national Hiroko Imai arrived in LaPorte to attend the inaugural semester, the only foreign student to enroll at PNC. From Osaka City, she was a graduate of Ogimachi High School, and planned to major in mathematics. Her journey to the U.S. had begun three years prior over a shared interest in stamp-collecting, when a friend of Hiroko had started a correspondence with Prof. Frederick R. Lisarelli, an associate professor of mechanical engineering at Purdue, after seeing his name in a Tokyo stamp-collector's newspaper. Unable to continue due to her unfamiliarity with English, Hiroko took up the correspondence, where she developed the desire to attend classes at Purdue. Hiroko was granted a two-year student visa residing with Lisarelli's family in LaPorte, though the Japanese government made it clear it wanted her to return home after her studies. To obtain her visa, Hiroko's father signed papers ensuring she would not marry or earn money in the U.S. Upon returning to Japan, Hiroko hoped to teach mathematics.[12]

An aura of transition and anticipation marked the year 1967. On Wednesday, May 31, Dean Schwarz officiated at a "Farewell to Barker" ceremony to mark the departure from the Michigan City mansion at the close of the final semester there for full-time students. The event was sponsored by the Student Executive Committee, the Men's Club, and the Women's Club, with students selecting Ronald P. Hendricks and Joanne M. Joseph as "Man of the Year" and "Woman of the Year." In August, after the summer session, a semi-formal dance was held in the mansion's garden; dubbed the "Final Farewell to Barker," the festivities were decorated with Japanese lanterns, the local Dick Anderson band providing the entertainment. The dance marked the end of an era, as moving preparations began in earnest for the coming semester. Referred to by university officials as "Operations M-Days," moving trucks carried away books, furniture, and lab equipment from the Barker Memorial Center and transported them to their new home at the Purdue North Central Regional Campus. The process was to be completed by August 21.[13]

Purdue North Central opened its doors for classes on September 13, 1967, at 8:00 am, to a student population of 1,135. Taking charge of the

From left: Dean of University Extension Charles Lawshe, University President Frederick Hovde, and Dean Robert Schwarz. (PNW Archives)

new facility was a group of eight administrators, including Schwarz, who remained the dean and director, with Prof. James R. Blackwell, a Marine Corps. and World War II combat veteran with degrees in Forestry, Political Science, and Business Administration, as assistant dean. The spacious new state-of-the-art "Education Building" required a redefinition of the institution which Schwarz was only too happy to provide: "We are trying to change our image from an extension to a campus.... Now we like to think of Purdue having five campuses – one of which just happens to be at [West] Lafayette."[14] The university employed 26 full-time faculty as classes got underway, along with a number of part-time lecturers. An official dedication ceremony took place on October 29, the last of a nine-day schedule of events that opened the campus to the press and public and culminated in a formal robed procession of Purdue officials led by President Hovde, who performed the dedication. In addition to the campus festivities, the Westville community welcomed the opening of PNC with celebrations of its own, including a dance held at Westville High School and a buffet prepared by the community for 55 faculty members at Hoovers restaurant on October 25. It was already evident, however, that the growth in demand for higher education in the area that had driven the establishment of PNC had not slowed, even as it began its first semester classes. Blackwell noted during the week of the dedication ceremony that the Education building was already at capacity, stating that "We've already found that this building isn't large enough to contain all of the classes at some times." Plans were already underway for the expansion necessary to meet future enrollment demands.[15]

Purdue North Central, often referred to as the "cornfield campus" by university officials, was uniquely positioned for expansion by virtue of its rural location, the only campus in the region not in an urban setting. It was evident from the beginning that university officials expected PNC to eventually become a four-year institution, although they were initially unwilling to say exactly when such a program would be created. However, enrollment figures—which were cited as a key determination in future plans—showed every indication of increasing. This was, in part, a continuation of the regional growth in population and economic opportunity that had seen enrollments rise at the Barker Memorial Center, but the new facility at PNC accelerated this trend by both increased capacity and appeal to a larger geographic area while offering higher education closer to home. It had been estimated during the early stages of the university's development that the student population could reach 1,200 by 1971, a figure that had almost been reached in the fall of 1967 and was quickly surpassed. Taking into account that spring enrollments are generally lower than fall, the second half of the 1968-69 school year still saw a 15 percent increase, with 1,116 students (981 undergraduate and 135 graduate students) compared to the prior year's total of 967. The year of 1969-70 began with 1,285 students and experienced only a small drop during the second half to 1,232—increases of approximately 8 percent and 10 percent respectively—and in September of 1970 the largest freshman class in PNC history attended orientation, part of a total enrollment of 1,515 for the 1970-71 session.[16]

The rise in student population further correlated with the steady expansion of course offerings. By September of 1969, for example, there were fourteen English courses available to undergraduate and graduate students, up from four only two years prior. The following year the curriculum grew with five new foreign language courses, allowing students to earn sixteen credits in Spanish or French, and thirteen in German. This was important not only as evidence of academic growth, but a further indication of the university working toward offering a broader range of degree programs, as language courses were a common requirement. These are examples only; similar additions occurred rapidly across nearly every discipline during the first five years at Purdue North Central, and were attributed to increased enrollment and retention rates.

In the annual report for 1969-70, the increased course offerings in the Humanities and Industrial Management were credited with a 25 percent increase in second-year students and a 206 percent jump in third-year students, while the following year saw not only a record number of freshman but an increase in retention from 50 percent to 66 percent due to the addition of upper level courses. In 1969 another, more visible symbol of PNC's academic expansion arrived in the form of a microwave TV receiving tower rising 120 feet above the surrounding farmland, offering a new form of educational integration between the four major state universities and their regional campuses through live and pre-recorded coursework. The cooperative initiative between Purdue, Ball State, Indiana, and Indiana State universities can be traced back to the early 1960s, having first been approved by the 95th Indiana General Assembly. At the 1964 Indiana Conference of Higher Education it had been suggested that "cooperative educational programs involving the state owned schools and private colleges be expanded," and "That increased emphasis be put on educational television as a means of extending educational opportunities," in addition to the establishment of new regional campuses. PNC was finally added to this network in August of 1969, offering three credit courses in its first semester of operation: Management Lectures, Introduction to Natural Resource Conservation, and Foods and Nutrition, the last of which was broadcast live with "talkback" capabilities to allow students to ask questions.

By 1971, this steady expansion of courses enabled PNC to offer the first two years of almost every Purdue degree program, in addition to seven Associate degrees.[17]

Plans for the expansion of campus facilities were underway prior to the beginning of classes in 1967 beginning with the completion of the original Education Building, which had been designed to accommodate an extension with minimal cost. The project—funded by university and federal grants at a cost of $675,000—was carried out by Tonn & Blank Inc., and added a total of 12,376 square feet of space to the building. Within the addition were classrooms and laboratory space, including a new $20,000 psychology lab located on the third floor. At the same time, the unfinished basement space—7,000 square feet—was developed to allow for an expansion of the library and relocation of the computer lab, while offering new student recreation space. This extension of the Education Building, completed in 1969, was only the first step in a larger plan for the North Central Campus. To accomplish this, the university hired the campus planning firm Johnson, Johnson, & Roy, Inc. of Ann Arbor, Michigan, to develop recommendations for a future campus able to accommodate a student body of 15,000. The first phase of development was the construction of a second building that would serve as one-third library space, and one-third classrooms, with the remaining space to be used as faculty offices. The university was in particular need of the new library facilities; the temporary library located in the Education Building was quickly reaching capacity with 20,000 volumes by 1971, making it necessary to put additional shelves in the adjacent student lounge area. As the original Education facility had been planned to be used exclusively as a science building, the construction of more classroom space allowed for the beginning of a transition of non-science courses to a new location.[18]

Purdue's centennial year of 1969 brought a host of activities and changes to campus. At a Centennial event in January, Governor Edgar D. Whitcomb asserted that "If Indiana is to achieve the destiny which must be hers, we must keep our institutions of higher education progressive and within the reach of all people." It was a clear message of support not only for the state's research institutions, but the regional campus concept that brought the expertise of the University within reach of its citizens throughout the state.

In February, L. O. Nelson, dean for student services and continuing education in West Lafayette and Kenneth L. Schwab, president of the Student Union board in West Lafayette, presented an official Purdue Centennial flag to the campus. The presentation symbolized the continuing concept of the University as a system of campuses, but more tangible changes would soon follow. On June 11 the campus held its first commencement exercises on the lawn in front of the Education Building. In September, the Purdue University Board of Trustees approved the designation of "School of General Studies" for PNC and the other regional campuses, allowing them to be more flexible in admission standards and giving them the authority to offer remedial courses not offered on the West Lafayette campus in order to better meet the needs of area residents.

The proposed new library building received approval by the Purdue University trustees in August of 1969 as part of a $23.5 million expansion budget for regional campus development. Construction was put on hold, however, as officials waited for the approval of the campus plan being developed by JJ&R and the firm's recommendation for a suitable location for the new building. Three alternate plans were ultimately presented to Purdue officials, the final master plan being accepted by the trustees at their meeting on April 26, 1972. At the meeting, Dr. Lawshe presented architectural drawings of the new building—now named the Library, Student, Faculty Building—and showed its proposed location to the gathered officials. Initial plans put the total cost of the 100,000 square foot building at $5.2 million, although this number was reduced somewhat after construction bids were taken in June to approximately $4.5 million. The project was able to begin the following month.[19]

During these years academic affairs flourished. In 1971 Dr. John J. Pappas founded the student literary journal *Portals*, with Dr. Barbara Lootens directing a student contest to identify contributors. In February 1972 Schwarz announced "Project Icarus," a program inspired by English chair Robert Ryan, allowing high school seniors in the top ten percent of their class and with Scholastic Aptitude Test scores of 1100 or

In 1969 Purdue University celebrated its centennial. Here Dean Robert Schwarz (right) is accepting the official centennial flag. (PNW Archives)

more to enroll in English courses at PNC for college credit. As a special incentive, if a student received a grade of "A" a local business would pay for the student's tuition and books. The spring of 1972 saw the addition of an "Afro-American History Week," a golf team playing its matches at the Beechwood course in LaPorte, the announcement of the first PNC annual golf tournament, and the completion of a campus master plan to accommodate 15,000 students. A milestone occurred in December 1968 with the accreditation of PNC's associate degree program by the National League of Nursing. An expanded engagement function included ten one-week management conferences for Midwest Steel Division of National Steel Corporation, five lectures on "American Political Parties and Pressure Groups" by faculty member and future state legislator Anita O. Bowser, and an enlarged non-credit schedule with Principles of Real Estate, Water Color Painting, Preparing Your State

The first commencement exercises convened on the lawn in front of the Education Building on June 11, 1969. Charles H. Lawshe, vice president for regional campuses, spoke to a crown of over 500 people before awarding five master's degrees, three baccalaureate degrees, 28 associate degrees and 43 certificates. (PNW Archives)

and Federal Income Tax Returns, and Radio Amateur License Preparation ranging in price from $10 to $35.[20]

As university officials looked to the future, the faculty and students of Purdue North Central prepared to enter a new decade. The first commencement held in the history of the new campus occurred on June 12, 1969, at 10:00 am, when seventy-nine students were awarded degrees and certificates on the campus lawn by Dr. Lawshe, who also provided the commencement address. The arrival of 1970 was a quiet one after the tremendous activity of the previous years, described in the *Herald-Argus* as a "year of reflection." While there were still many developments occurring at the administrative level, to the students and local communities it was the first year in which no major projects were underway in Westville. Student life was still developing. The LaPorte newspaper found that there had been an "indifference to PNC activities

With the advent of intercollegiate athletics came the first cheerleading squad in 1969. In this photograph from 1971, PNC cheerleader letters were presented (from left) to Linda Starkey, Jackie Timm, Janet Borg, Patricia Gallagher and Carol Jankowski. (PNW Archives)

and clubs" from the inception of the campus due to its nature as a "commuter campus." Interestingly, this same factor spared PNC from the political protest and violence that had occurred elsewhere in the country. Schwarz stated in September of 1970 that students hoping to organize "activist-type programs" faced a number of obstacles; not only did students go home every evening, many worked, leaving little time for political agitation. In addition, PNC's two-year programs meant there was a "fast turnover of students." Pointing out that PNC had not experienced any unrest, Schwarz stated that "We cannot allow the university to become a propaganda platform for certain people." Still, there were occasional demonstrations, though small and peaceful. In May of 1970, "less than two dozen" students tried to gather support for a campus strike in response to the deaths of six students who had been killed by members of the Ohio National Guard at Kent State University while protesting the bombing of Cambodia. The PNC students stated they were "responding to a request by the National Student Association that students and faculty members suspend normal activities until the occupation of Kent State ceases." However, the majority of students remained in class.[21]

A further major focus in the development of PNC's plans for the future was the preparation for a visit by the North Central Association Accreditation Team in the spring of 1971 for the purpose of receiving "operationally separate accreditation." Up to that point, PNC—and its predecessor at the Barker Memorial Center—had been operating under a "blanket" accreditation of Purdue University by the North Central Association of Colleges and Secondary Schools. The Association's executive board voted on March 23, 1969, to authorize an examination of PNC and appointed Dean Robert Ray of the University of Iowa as a consultant to assist the faculty and administration in Westville. Schwarz appointed Assistant Dean Blackwell to conduct an analysis of PNC and the preparation of a "Self-Study" to present to the Association. To achieve this, "campus operations were divided into seven major areas and plans were made to appoint seven special committees to research and prepare appropriate portions of the Self-Study report," while a Steering Committee—with Schwarz as chair and composed of the chairs of six other committees—would then compile the various chapters into a final report. A memorandum from the Office of the Dean dated February 13, 1970, explained that the review by the North Central Association would be at the "Associate level only," including the two-year programs that worked toward a bachelor's degree to be completed at another campus. This was an important step in PNC's expansion toward being able to offer four-year programs as "Preliminary accreditation for baccalaureate programs cannot be taken until after accreditation for the two year program is granted." A visitation team of the Association appeared in April of 1971 and spent two-and-a-half days conducting interviews with faculty and students, ultimately recommending that Purdue North Central be granted operationally separate accreditation; this was granted in July and made effective in September for the freshman and sophomore year. PNC had come of age, being recognized by its peers as a viable degree-granting institution.

With this triumph, Schwarz announced his retirement from administrative responsibilities to return to teaching. Speaking of his decision,

Schwarz stated that he had waited to step down "because there were several important projects which I wanted to see completed." These included—in addition to the original Education building that would one day bear his name—"the North Central Association accreditation this past summer; the establishment of a master plan for campus development which will be released shortly, and the planning for the second building is now well under way after being funded by the 1971 General Assembly." Schwarz remained a member of the PNC faculty as an instructor, and continued to carry out public relations and development responsibilities for the university. It would be difficult to describe his term at the helm of Purdue North Central as anything less than immensely successful.

Schwarz's remarkable tenure witnessed exceptional growth from a tenuous extension site in an English mansion to an accredited two-year institution with a growing enrollment of over 1,500, expanded academic degree programs, ongoing engagement activities linking the campus with the community, approval of the construction of a second building and every prospect for future success. The transition in leadership to Prof. John W. Tucker, vice president of the University of Utah, announced in June of 1972, brought a symbolic end of an era in the history of Purdue North Central, as the campus firmly established itself as an important institution of higher learning in Northwest Indiana capable of meeting the region's educational needs for decades to come, with the promise of transforming into a fully-fledged, degree-granting university clearly visible on the horizon.[22]

---

[1] "Purdue's Hovde Compares Area Campus to 'Original,'" April 20, 1967, News Releases PNC, Box 1, Folder 10, PNW Archives.

[2] Frederick L. Hovde, "Purdue University," in "Purdue University North Central Institutional Self-Study, 1970" (Westville: Purdue North Central, 1970), I-1.

[3] *News-Dispatch* (Michigan City, IN), February 21, 1962, News-clippings PNC, Box 1, Folder 11, PNW Archives; *News-Dispatch*, July 30, 1964, News-clippings PNC, Box 1, Folder 13, PNW Archives; *Exponent* (Lafayette, IN), May 24, 1962, News-clippings PNC, Box 1, Folder 11, PNW; "Purchase of Property for a North Central Campus," May 21, 1962,

News Releases PNC, Box 1, Folder 3, PNW Archives.

[4] *Indicator* (Westville, IN), April 11, 1963; *Herald-Argus*, (LaPorte, IN), June 10, 1963, News-clippings PNC, Box 1, Folder 12, PNW Archives.

[5] Board of Trustees minutes, 1964 May 29, Purdue University Libraries Archives and Special Collections.

[6] *News-Dispatch*, May 12, 1964, News-clippings PNC, Box 1, Folder 13, PNW Archives.

[7] *News-Dispatch*, July 30, 1964; *Star* (Terre Haute, IN), Sept. 10, 1964; *Indicator*, Oct. 22, 1964, News-clippings PNC, Box 1, Folder 13, PNW Archives.

[8] *Herald-Argus*, April 6, 1965, News-clippings PNC, Box 1, Folder 14, PNW Archives; Board of Trustee minutes, May 5, 1965, Purdue University Libraries, Archives and Special Collections, Lafayette, Indiana.

[9] *News-Dispatch*, June 28, 1965; *Herald-Argus*, June 28, 1965, News-clippings PNC, Box 1, Folder 14, PNW Archives.

[10] *Vidette-Messenger* (Valparaiso, IN), Oct. 20, 1967, Historical PNC Collection, Unprocessed, PNW Archives.

[11] *Herald-Argus*, Nov. 19, 1965; "New Computer Technology Program," May 29, 1967, News Releases PNC, Box 1, Folder 10, PNW Archives.

[12] *Vidette-Messenger*, July 11, 1966, and *Herald-Press* (St. Joseph, MI), Oct. 13, 1966, News-clippings PNC, Box 1, Folder 15, PNW Archives; *Post-Tribune*, (Gary, IN), Aug. 3, 1967, and *Herald-Argus*, Aug. 3, 1967, News-clippings PNC, Box 1, Folder 17, PNW Archives.

[13] "Farewell to Barker," May 23, 1967, "Moving to New Campus," July 21, 1967, and "Farewell Dance," July 28, 1967, News Releases PNC, Box 1, Folder 10, NW Archives.

[14] Ibid.

[15] *Indicator*, Oct. 19, 1967; *Indianapolis Star*, Oct. 20, 1967; *News-Dispatch*, Oct. 23, 1967; *Herald-Argus*, Oct. 26, 1967; Historical PNC Collection, Unprocessed, PNW Archives.

[16] *Herald-Argus*, March 1, 1969, News-clippings PNC, Box 1, Folder 22, PNW Archives; *Herald-Argus*, March 12, 1970, News-clippings PNC, Box 1, Folder 25, PNW Archives; *Indicator*, Oct. 30, 1969, News-clippings PNC, Box 1, Folder 23, PNW Archives; *News-Dispatch*, Sept. 16, 1970, News-clippings PNC, Box 1, Folder 26, PNW Archives; Purdue University Regional Campus Administration Annual Report 1970-1971 (Lafayette: Purdue University, 1971), Section 5, 3.

[17] *Herald-Argus*, July 31, 1969; Purdue University Regional Campus Administration Annual Report 1969-70 (Lafayette: Purdue University, 1970),

Section 5, 3; Purdue University Regional Campus Administration Annual Report 1970-71 (Lafayette: Purdue University, 1971), Section 5, 3; *News-Dispatch*, May 12, 1964, News-clippings PNC, Box 1, Folder 13, PNW Archives; *Herald-Argus*, August 22, 1969, News-clippings PNC, Box 1, Folder 23, PNW Archives.

[18] *Indianapolis Star*, Oct. 20, 1967; *News-Dispatch*, Aug. 14, 1969, News-clippings PNC, Box 1, Folder 23, PNW Archives; Purdue University Regional Campus Administration Annual Report 1969-70 (Lafayette: Purdue University, 1970), Section 5, 8; Purdue University Regional Campus Administration Annual Report 1970-71 (Lafayette: Purdue University, 1971), Section 5, 10.

[19] Board of Trustees minutes, May 26, 1972, Purdue University Libraries, Archives and Special Collections, Lafayette, Indiana; Purdue University Regional Campus Administration Annual Report 1970-71 (Lafayette: Purdue University, 1971), Section 5, 10; *News-Dispatch*, June 12, 1972, News-clippings PNC, Unprocessed, PNW Archives.

[20] "Section II—Analysis of Self-Study Reports," in "Regional Campus Summary Report: North Central Self-Study July 1, 1971" (Lafayette: Purdue University, 1971), 10; Appendix Z, "Organization for the Self-Study," in Purdue University North Central Campus NCA Accreditation Data, 1970 (Westville: Purdue University, 1970), XI-107; Administrative Memorandum 3-70, February 13, 1970, in "Purdue University North Central Campus NCA Accreditation Data, 1970" (Westville: Purdue University, 1970), XI-109.

[21] *Indicator*, June 12, 1969, News-clippings PNC, Box 1, Folder 23, PNW Archives; *Herald-Argus*, Oct. 2, 1970, News-clippings PNC, Box 1, Folder 27, PNW Archives; *News-Dispatch*, May 7, 1970, News-clippings PNC, Box 1, Folder 25, PNW Archives; *News-Dispatch*, Sept. 2, 1970, News-clippings PNC, Box 1, Folder 26, PNW Archives.

[22] *Vidette-Messenger*, Oct. 28, 1971, News-clippings PNC, Box 1, Folder 29, PNW Archives; *Herald-Argus*, June 26, 1972, News-clippings PNC, Unprocessed, PNW Archives.

THE TUCKER-FULLER YEARS: 1972-1982

Jackie Perkins

After coming through the uncertain early years of establishing a new Purdue campus, the leaders and staff of Purdue University North Central began to look toward the future as they made plans to boost both the school and, in keeping with the University's Land Grant mission, the community that surrounded it. One of the principal changes taking place at this time was the appointment of a new chancellor following the resignation of Dean and Director Robert F. Schwarz in late 1971.[1] An Advisory Committee was created to aid in the search for a new campus administrator while staff and students continued to open PNC to the community that existed both within and around the campus.[2]

In early February of 1972, PNC planned a week-long event to celebrate Afro-American History Week.[3] The event was promoted as a way "to provide the North Central community with an insight into the culture and history of Afro-Americans, as well as to pay tribute to a segment of the American population that has made an enormous contribution to the country's prosperity and also played a major role in determining the character of the nation."[4] This week-long event was open to both the students and the public and included specially themed programs and lectures for local elementary and secondary students. These included Afro-American culture and history exhibits as well as discussions and lectures from representatives of the Frank, London, Brown Historical Association.[5] The week wrapped up with a dance, "Soul Extravaganza," that had special entertainment from a dance group as well as a performance by Prince Matonga, a dancer from the Bahamas.[6] The week was considered a huge success with an estimated 600 people, including elementary and secondary students, taking advantage of the events.[7]

Even as the staff of PNC began making steps toward the future, so did others on campus. Students became disappointed in the content of the school newspaper, *The Observer*, and decided it was time to start their own paper which they named *OBII*.[8] The topics in the new publication were decided by student staff members and covered things such as "sex, religion, dope, rock music, the draft, the environment and other items in which youth are interested."[9] The newspaper was filled not only with the more controversial topics but also with humor and helpful hints on day to day activities.[10] Theresa Russo, a junior sociology major, explained the student reaction to the first issue of the newspaper:

> A lot of kids expected more. There was no obscenities or blasts at the school administration. We wanted to take it easy at first; give the administration a chance. The overall reaction, though, by students was good. Many kids want to write for us and that's one of *OBII*'s purposes: to be a showcase for artistic and writing talents.[11]

Russo also commented on the free reign given to the paper by the school saying, "We don't have any guidelines and I hope they don't give us any, we wouldn't follow them. I expect they'll get uptight and excited when we put sex in the paper."[12]

Students speaking through this new paper was only the beginning as only one month later students gathered to speak out about what they referred to as "shabby treatment by the PNC administration to the students."[13] Dean James Blackwell was present at the meeting to gather the complaints for Schwarz. The two major concerns given at the meeting were the hours of the campus game room and the plans for the spring weekend folk festival.[14] Though no resolution to these issues was mentioned, it is nonetheless impressive to see the willingness of the administration to listen to the students when members of the student body registered complaints.

As PNC began making strides toward opening the campus to more students from the community, plans also had to be made to expand the available space. In early May of 1972, the Board of Trustees of Purdue University began accepting bids for the construction of the second building on PNC's campus.[15] According to Schwarz, the new building would be "one-third library, one-third classrooms and offices, and one-third student services such as book stores, lounges, and other facilities."[16] Following this, Schwarz released the master plan for the PNC campus. The plan by Johnson, Johnson and Roy, Inc., called for "an ultimate size of 15,000 students" with the focus on the creation of a commuter campus.[17] The plan also called for a campus that "would include 2.1 million square feet of building space, including a gym, auditorium, student-faculty building, library, faculty offices, labs, administrative facilities and class-rooms."[18] This master plan would be the last major report from Schwarz as only one month later the Board named a new campus administrator, Dr. John Tucker of the University of Utah.[19]

John W. Tucker received his bacca-laureate in English from Brigham Young University in 1951, his mas-ter's degree in guidance and coun-seling from Arizona State in 1952, and his doctorate from Harvard Uni-versity in 1957. (PNW Archives)

One of the first announcements from the new chancellor came at a meeting where Tucker proclaimed the following six educational goals that PNC would aim to accomplish:

- Non-credit classes.
- Short duration certificate courses emphasizing marketable skills.
- Course of longer duration; one- and two-year associate de-gree programs.
- Other associate degree two-year programs which are now offered at PNC and can be expanded.
- Limited bachelor of arts and sciences degree programs de-signed to meet the needs of this locality.
- Graduate classes in such fields as teaching which will allow master's degree people to continue their work-a-day tasks while continuing their training.[20]

In 1974 a group of Michigan City business owners arranged this "Information Office on Wheels" for PNC to travel to the various communities in its service region to make the general public more aware of the educational opportunities available in its own back yard. (PNW Archives)

Following this announcement, it became clear that PNC was making strong strides towards offering a college education to everyone in the community. In 1973 Tucker's title changed to "chancellor." Under his continuing leadership the campus added new student activities, programs, and community linkages. Baseball became a varsity sport in the spring of 1978. Athletics were an important adjunct to the campus, providing opportunities for student leadership and physical exercise, while at the same time raising the institution's profile in the local community through newspaper coverage of the games. Cultural and intellectual life benefited from continuing lecture and artist events including appearances on campus of nationally-known figures such as pollster George Gallop and inventor R. Buckminster Fuller. In the fall of 1973 three new programs, a Child Care Center, a Mini College, and the Bridge Program, began. The Child Care Center offered two-hour periods of child care for students taking courses at PNC.[21] The Mini College was operated on successive weekends and offered a limited num-

Dedicated on March 21, 1975, the new Library-Student-Faculty Building added 100,000 square feet of space for a library, offices, classrooms, bookstore, listening room, microfilm room, group study rooms, audio-visual services, a conference room, food services, and student recreational areas. (PNW Archives)

ber of courses to adult students who were unable to attend class during the week.[22] The most extensive of the three new programs was the Bridge Program:

> The Bridge Program was created by the Community College to aid students who do not meet the entrance requirements of regular Purdue curricula. It is basically a two-semester sequence of "make-up" or remedial courses. The courses are not accredited by any special group or association, and many of the credits, because of the remedial nature of the courses, are not transferable to other institutions or to other programs at Purdue.
>
> The strength of the Bridge Program is in its ability to enable students, deficient in some way, to enter [a] regular curriculum. Through courses and counseling, one of three possible objectives is achieved with each student assigned to the Bridge Program: (1) the student becomes prepared to enter and succeed

in the regular curriculum for which he/she originally applied;
(2) the student is prepared to enter a new or different program,
one that is in keeping with his skills, interests and potential success; and (3) the student is made aware of his or her limitations
with regards to higher education and is helped to locate other,
non-college alternatives.[23]

Tucker's time as chancellor of PNC were years of growth and
change. The new structure, the Library-Student-Faculty Building, or
LSF for short, opened for classes in the spring of 1975. LSF was designed with space devoted to offices, food service, classrooms, student
recreational areas and a library.[24] The opening of the new building
came at an opportune time as Tucker explained:

> Purdue North Central is not faced with the problem of de-
> clining enrollments as are many institutions of higher educa-
> tion. Conversely, many students are deciding to stay at home
> because of the economic squeeze and our enrollments are in-
> creasing. We expect continued growth at about 10% per year.
> With the opening of our new building and approval pending on
> several new programs to be offered, the outlook of 1975 is
> bright. While many other institutions are confronted with prob-
> lems of retrenchment, we are looking forward to growth.[25]

Tucker was correct in this statement as enrollment in the fall of
1974 showed a seven percent increase and the enrollment for the spring
of 1975 was up 17.4 percent from the previous year.[26] Even with its
increasing enrollment numbers, PNC continued its tradition of providing strong community outreach through its curriculum:

> PNC's strong curriculum includes industrial management,
> industrial supervision and industrial engineering technology
> programs. Through the School of Technology, two-year associ-
> ate degrees in such areas as industrial engineering technology,
> mechanical engineering technology, computer technology, fore-
> manship, civil engineering technology and electrical engineer-
> ing technology are available. In the last year PNC has devel-
> oped a new credit curriculum specifically designed to serve area
> businesses. The secretarial arts program was initiated in the fall

and is designed to develop the executive level secretary for area businesses.[27]

In addition to the programs aimed at local businesses, PNC also planned courses and workshops for area businesses and industries including "Digital Electronics for Bendix of South Bend; Principles of Management for Hedwin of LaPorte; Clark Management Club Program for Clark Equipment of Michigan City; and Staff Training for Citizens Bank of Michigan City. PNC also held a workshop on Creativity in Management which was attended by representatives from the following: Tom & Blank, Society Lingerie, First Merchants National Bank, Jim's Supermarkets, Teledyne Casting Service, Chicago South Shore and South Bend Railroad, Arno Adhesives, Dispatch Publishing Company, Whirlpool Corporation, United States Steel and Thermium Company of Highland, Indiana."[28] Other courses were added to the campus offerings for local business and industry.[29]

Dr. William R. Fuller succeeded Tucker as interim chancellor. Prior to his appointment he was the acting vice chancellor for academic services at PNC.[30] One of the first changes that Fuller brought was the creation of the Chancellor's Advisory Board. The purpose of this Board was to obtain advice and counsel from community residents on how PNC could continue to provide for the educational needs of the community.[31] The Board also advised Fuller on academic programs, campus development, and gave a community perspective on what the campus' future priorities should be.[32] Fuller also oversaw establishment of the PNC Alumni Association with 556 charter members in 1981. The new group quickly became active sponsoring a post-commencement reception, the annual golf outing, homecoming celebrations, and other social activities.

Fuller had the privilege of announcing another major milestone in the development of the campus on May 9, 1980, when the Indiana Commission on Higher Education (ICHE) approved the establishment of a Bachelor of Science in Supervision, the first baccalaureate degree to be offered by PNC. Designed to provide career mobility opportunities for working adults in the area's steel mills, over time the flexible nature of the degree, and its practical orientation, found ready acceptance by workers in a number of industries who found they could

William R. Fuller served as interim chancellor from 1979 to 1982, presiding over implementation of the first baccalaureate degree, establishment of the Chancellor's Advisory Board, and the founding of the PNC Alumni Association. (PNW Archives)

enhance their knowledge and employment options by enrolling in evening or weekend classes while maintaining their normal work routine.[33] Tucker would continue to steer PNC on this path of outreach and community involvement through his next four years as chancellor until his resignation in 1979.[34]

In September of 1981, ICHE approved a Bachelor of Liberal Studies degree. A general studies curriculum aimed at working adults who needed a degree for career advancement, the new program proved a popular supplement to the more technically-oriented B.S. in Supervision program.[35] According to Fuller, "this four-year Liberal Studies degree program will provide the student with a broad exposure to the humanities, social sciences, physical sciences, mathematics and technology, with each student having wide latitude in the choice of scientific, technical or non-technical options to supplement a base of humanistic studies."[36] The addition of these new degrees opened new opportunities for the PNC community. An institutional self-study released in 1981 noted that PNC offered options to students who might not otherwise be able to take advantage of the University.[37] This self-study also noted that the emphasis at PNC had been on the following:

- Freshman and sophomore transfer curricula offered by the University that lead to a Bachelor of Science or Bachelor of Arts degree;

Community groups frequently used the new campus for meetings. Located in the center of the competing cities of LaPorte, Michigan City, Chesterton and Valparaiso, PNC earned the nickname "Little Switzerland" because it was considered "neutral territory." This 1979 meeting includes (from left) William Fuller, Robert Miller, Robert Schwarz and A. J. Rumley. (PNW Archives)

- Associate degree curricula in Nursing, General Business, Secretarial Arts, and various fields of Technology;

- Programs, conferences and short courses related to the interests of the people in the neighboring communities for the purpose of general education or occupational advancement;

- Development education through the Community College, with a liberalized admissions policy to prepare students for admission to the program of their choice;

- Selected graduate courses in a limited number of subject-matter fields.[38]

Shortly after confirmation of the second new baccalaureate degree at PNC, Fuller announced his resignation as chancellor, explaining:

I am currently within a few months of completing four years at the North Central campus. During three of these I have served as its Chancellor and during this period, the campus and certain community leaders have reviewed several charges presented by the President of Purdue University upon my appointment to the Chancellorship and have in general fulfilled at least the short-term content of those charges. I am rather proud of our accomplishments during this period. In my opinion, the remaining goals of the campus, and there are many – some yet to be identified, are of a long-term nature and require a sustained leadership. Accordingly, I have suggested to President Hansen, and he has accepted, the idea that the interim leadership phase at Purdue North Central should be ended.[39]

Though Fuller served the shortest tenure of any PNC chancellor, his efforts helped to bring about the first two bachelor degrees for the campus and the creation of the Chancellor's Advisory Board.[40]

In the ten years of leadership under Tucker and Fuller, significant changes took place at the slowly growing "Campus in the Cornfield," moving it into the ranks of institutions offering baccalaureate degrees, greatly increasing engagement activities through the institution's continuing education programs and creation of the Chancellor's Advisory Board and PNC Alumni Association, and adding nearly a thousand new students to the annual enrollment. Both made the needs of the community their primary focus and did their best to create programs that allowed more members of the community to enter the university. This focus on community helped to aid the continuous climb in enrollment that PNC experienced in not only the full- and part-time student admissions but also in the Community College. In the fall of 1980, the Community College was the largest school at PNC with 595 students enrolled, and two years later total enrollment reached a record high of 2,544.[41] These numbers show that both Tucker and Fuller understood what was needed in the community during that time, an accessible way for local community members to further their education. When Fuller left the chancellorship in June 1982, the institution was poised to begin a new phase of expansion.

[1] "Dean Selection Group Meets," *Vidette-Messenger* (Valparaiso, IN), December 8, 1971.

[2] Ibid.

[3] "PNC to Observe Afro-American History Week," *Vidette-Messenger*, February 3, 1972.

[4] Ibid.

[5] Ibid.

[6] Ibid.

[7] "PNC Officials Elated Over Afro Week Events," *Herald-Argus* (LaPorte, IN), February 21, 1972.

[8] "PNC Paper Seeks 'Relevance,'" *News-Dispatch* (Michigan City, IN), March 11, 1972

[9] Ibid.

[10] Ibid.

[11] Ibid.

[12] Ibid. In 1976 the first one-page issue of a new student newspaper, the *Spectator*, appeared.

[13] "Shabby Treatment by PNC Administration is Charged," *News-Dispatch*, April 29, 1972.

[14] Ibid.

[15] "PNC Bidding 2nd Building Announced," *Herald-Argus*, May 12, 1972.

[16] Ibid.

[17] "Plans for Developing PNC are Announced," *News-Dispatch*, May 24, 1972.

[18] Ibid.

[19] "New Dean named at PNC," *News-Dispatch*, June 26, 1972.

[20] "PNC Education Looks at Future Programs," *Herald-Argus*, January 16, 1973.

[21] "Child Care Center," Aug. 14, 1973, Press Release Collection, PNW Archives.

[22] "PNC's First Mini College," October 3, 1973, Press Release Collection, PNW Archives.

[23] "The Institutional Self-Study of Purdue University North Central Campus" (Westville, IN: Purdue North Central, 1981), C-64-C-65, PNW Archives.

[24] "Purdue North Central to Dedicate New Library-Student-Faculty Building," March 10, 1975, Press Release Collection, PNW Archives.

[25] "Outlook of Purdue North Central," March 10, 1975, Press Release Col-

lection, PNW Archives.

[26] Ibid.

[27] "Purdue North Central and the Communities," March 10, 1975, Press Release Collection, NW Archives.

[28] Ibid.

[29] Ibid.

[30] "Prof. William R. Fuller Appointed as Interim Chancellor," March 27, 1979, Press Release Collection, PNW Archives.

[31] "Chancellor's Advisory Board," August 10, 1979, Press Release Collection, PNW Archives.

[32] Ibid.

[33] "Purdue University Approves Actions for Purdue North Central," May 28, 1975, Press Release Collection, PNW Archives.

[34] "Two Bachelor Degrees Approved," May 9,1980, Press Release Collection, PNW Archives.

[35] "New Bachelor of Liberal Studies Confirmed," September 9, 1981, Press Release Collection, PNW Archives.

[36] Ibid.

[37] "Institutional Self-Study" (1981), C-1.

[38] Ibid.

[39] "Chancellor's Resignation," December 9, 1981, Press Release Collection, PNW Archives.

[40] Ibid.

[41] "Institutional Self-Study" (1981), C-67

"HE BLED BLACK AND OLD GOLD": THE ALSPAUGH YEARS, 1981-1999

Edward Michael Rosary

INTRODUCTION

The *Oxford Dictionary* defines an engineer as "a person who de-signs, builds, or maintains engines, machines, or structures."[1] There is no doubt that Dale Alspaugh was an engineer, both by degree and in his work at Purdue University North Central. Alspaugh is the man largely responsible for engineering the success of PNC from a school with 2,293 students and only one baccalaureate program in 1981, to 3,355 students and six baccalaureate degrees at the time of his retirement in 1999.[2]

Engineering was certainly in Dale Alspaugh's blood, and he was described as a man who "bled black and gold." Alspaugh earned his Engineering Sciences' PhD from Purdue University in 1965. He imme-diately began teaching at the school of Aeronautics and Astronautics that same year. Alspaugh would continue instructing potential future astronauts until 1981. No public school has graduated more astronauts than Purdue, a program Alspaugh contributed to as both a student and then a faculty member from 1959 until 1981. After twenty-two years at Purdue West Lafayette, Alspaugh embarked on a journey that would not take him to the frontiers of space, but instead to rural LaPorte Coun-ty, Indiana.

EDUCATION FOR WORKING ADULTS

On June 15, 1981, Dale Alspaugh began his career at Purdue North Central as Vice Chancellor. At the time of his arrival, PNC offered just one baccalaureate program, focusing primarily on short-term programs for working adults due to the average student age of 26. In fact, 70 per-cent of students only took one or two classes per semester. As part of PNC's belief in educating older working adults, it provided child care services to assist college parents.

The University also focused on offering courses that could be taken off campus at various locations including the Portage Adult Learning

Center, St. Anthony Hospital in Michigan City, LaPorte Hospital, Knox High School, and the Senior Citizen Center in LaPorte. Satellites were an important factor in attracting working adults. The Portage Adult Learning Center offered courses in supervision, psychology, English and accounting for just over $100. The Westville campus would continue to service the community's working professionals by adding a Real Estate Licensing course in the summer, as well as a special program for nurses in the fall of 1982. The University also included nighttime and weekend undergraduate courses, as well as graduate level courses for its sole graduate degree, a Master of Arts in Education in 1981.

On October 6, 1983, PNC began offering a course both for credit and non-credit, in cooperation with the PBS thirteen-part documentary series "Vietnam: A Television History." Among its other non-credit classes were Dancerobic, College for Kids, Typing, Real Estate Sales, Asbestos Training Program, Kick Your Bad Habits, CPA classes, Programing Microcomputers, How to Study in College, Self-hypnosis, Buying a Camera, travel courses, a course for senior citizen drivers, couses on plants, and even a class on becoming a clown.

ENROLLMENT

By June 1982, Alspaugh began his greatest engineering feat, that of altering the form and future of Purdue North Central and Northwest Indiana. Budgetary concerns somewhat subsided, as Alspaugh's positive outlook was correct and PNC saw record enrollment for the 1982 fall semester: 2,544 students, a 10.9 percent increase over the previous fall. This was a 115 percent increase since the university moved to the Westville campus fifteen years previously and met original enrollment projections in the 1972 report. PNC continued to set new attendance records in the spring of 1983, which saw its largest number of enrollments ever for a single registration period with 560 people passing through the registration lines, some standing in line to register six hours before it opened. That same semester would also see a 91 percent retention rate from the previous semester. This trend of record setting enrollment continued throughout the Alspaugh years, with fall semesters setting records for attendance until 1993. Though facing a slight enrollment decline in the spring of 1986, the following spring again set a record for enrollment, despite declining student populations throughout the rest of American colleges and universities. Much of this had to do with Alspaugh's constant emphasis on integrating PNC within the community, and as an establishment for working adults within the community.[3]

When Alspaugh arrived at PNC in 1981, farm income in Indiana was $4.3 billion, coming from 89,000 farms with 17 million acres

Dale W. Alspaugh received his M.E. degree from the University of Cincinnati, with M.S. and Ph.D. degrees in engineering from Purdue University. As a faculty member of the School of Aeronatuics and Astronautics at Purdue, he authored publications in the fields of flight and orbit mechanics and optimization. He came to PNC in 1981 as vice chancellor for academic services.

tilled. In total, the value of farmland in Indiana was about $27 billion. The state raised $2.85 billion in revenues and $1.7 billion in taxes against $2.85 in spending. Alspaugh, who had spent his prior career teaching prospective astronauts to reach for the stars, viewed Indiana as, "not a farming, nor a government state," noting that, "farm income was only three to six percent of the state wages, while manufacturing took up nearly forty percent. Farming is an important component, but there are a lot of others." Alspaugh's outlook on Indiana stated that, "The era of service is coming. It is becoming more and more important." Alspaugh further continued, "Industry will be here. Indiana is a manufacturing state, a bender of metal. Steel is our biggest industry."[4] Though he did not see the region as a future hub of technology, Alspaugh saw the importance of technology and education in Northwest Indiana.

The challenge was no easy task as Indiana High School students averaged 100 less points than their Midwest counterparts on Scholastic Achievement Test scores. In fact, in 1983 Indiana ranked 47th amongst states for proportion of residents who had completed at least four years of college. Making matters even worse was the fact that Indiana was losing those who were educated, as evidenced by the fact only 55,000 of 152,000 Purdue graduates resided in Indiana. The situation in PNC's own LaPorte County was even worse as only ten percent of residents over 25 had graduated from college, with sixteen percent not even completing high school between 1970 and 1980.

The problem with Indiana high school graduation rates would carry into the next decade. In 1990, college attendance among recent high

"A Silver Past ... A Golden Future" was the theme of PNC's celebration in 1992 of the 25th anniversary of the opening of the Westville campus. Activities took place throughout the year to mark the occasion. (PNW Archives)

school graduates was more than five percent below the national average. Alspaugh feared Indiana's future would be directly tied to its college graduates. Hoping to show the state the importance of education to Indiana's future, in a rare and unheard-of move, the presidents of Indiana's seven state-assisted universities joined to issue a challenge to the State of Indiana. Their challenge proposed a plan called "A Commitment to Quality," with the goals of increasing access, quality, and success. However, by March of 1991 the Indiana House of Representatives approved legislation that would cut roughly $15 million from Indiana's seven state universities from 1991 to 1993. Although the plan would still provide PNC with the same amount of money it previously had, it did not factor in inflation or enrollment growth. Fortunately, Alspaugh seemed ready to take on the task of educating Hoosiers. As an engineer Alspaugh recognized that, "You need a complete plan," especially in a recession.[5]

Alspaugh's successes as acting Chancellor in 1982-1983 led to his confirmation as permanent chancellor in February 1984. Alspaugh would continue the plan he started, often writing articles in local newspapers. These articles almost always highlighted the importance of higher education in a technologically evolving world. Alspaugh was not alone in this push however, as it coincided with a state-wide plan in which the week of January 15, 1984 was declared "Educate Indiana Week" by Governor Robert Orr. Throughout the state, commercials and newspapers ran ads signifying the importance of higher education. Alspaugh highlighted a Chicago *Sun-Times* article headlined, "College May Be Worth A Million," which quoted a Census Bureau study that suggested a college graduate was likely to earn nearly a million dollars more than a worker with just a high school diploma. Alspaugh also discussed how college graduates were less likely to be laid off, instead securing longer-lasting job security. Alspaugh believed that much of the reason for a lack of college education was simply fears of difficulty, age, gender, affordability, and being part of a culture that had avoided college. Realizing that the key to a successful PNC lay in the campus's ability to recruit working adults, Alspaugh highlighted facts that would appeal to that group. Some of the statistics included the fact that 69 percent of PNC's 2,400 students attended on a part-time basis. He also noted that 60 percent of students were female and highlighted the 1982 women's conference "Return to Learn." For those fearing they were too old, Alspaugh pointed out that the average age of the PNC student population was 27.1 years, and it was not uncommon to see not just mothers, but grandmothers at commencement.[6]

Having become chancellor, Alspaugh was able to start enacting his plans for PNC in 1983. Alspaugh and Purdue University President Steven C. Beering had their eyes set on strengthening the future of Indiana through strong regional campuses. These programs appeared to retain graduates within Indiana, as evidenced by PNC in which 86 percent of alumni continued to reside in Indiana. This trend continued until at least 1992 when three-quarters of the 4,000 surveyed PNC alumni resided within 40 miles of the campus. Over 90 percent remained in the state of Indiana.[7]

In 1982, another major concern surfaced. Only 3.4 percent of the student body was African-American, despite its primary source of enrollment being from Michigan City, which had a 17.6 percent black population. In 1987, 4.5 percent of PNC students were minorities, which rose to 6.8 percent in Fall 1991. Two years later enrollment dropped one percent from the previous year. This was the first drop in fall enrollment in fourteen years. The university did, however, achieve record highs in full-time students (15 percent), and minority student enrollment (8 percent). In the fall semester of 1999, Alspaugh's final term, PNC achieved record enrollments in full-time (1,734) students,

The Purdue North Central Alumni Association prepared its float for the annual July 4th parade to reference Purdue symbols including the "Boilermaker Special," synonymous with Purdue athletics, and the "All American Marching Band," a space shuttle reminiscent of Purdue's title as "Mother of Astronauts," and the marking of the 25th anniversary of the PNC campus. (PNW Archives)

surpassing part-time (1,621) enrollment for the first time. Three percent of the student body was African-American, two percent Hispanic, 93 percent Caucasian, and two percent other. When Alspaugh arrived, 70 percent of students took just one or two classes. Perhaps it was destiny that Alspaugh's final semester would achieve the goal of having more full-time than part-time students.

When Alspaugh was appointed in 1981, there were around 2,200 students and 50 faculty members. By 1990, There were around 3,400 students and only 70 professors. With Alspaugh's projections for 5,000 students by the turn of the millennium, something needed to be done to decrease the students-to-faculty ratio. To prepare for the influx of students, a plan for a third major building costing roughly $15 million was on the table to open in 1994. The building would consist of classrooms, laboratories and offices. The school also set its sights on a fourth major building to be opened in 2000 as Alspaugh hoped to add additional four -year programs.

The fifty percent increase in enrollment during his tenure was certainly a credit to Alspaugh's leadership. He envisioned a campus with more four-year programs, additional parking lots (much needed as security was being forced to guide students to parking spots in the grass), a new technology and robotics lab to be added in 1985, additional buildings planned to be built between 1987-1989, as well as a fourth building between 1991-1993. Alspaugh's plans were for an Indiana built on technological training and re-education. What began as offerings of computers in classrooms in 1982 would finally culminate in 1995 with the construction of the Technology Building. PNC's emphasis on technology classes would be one of its strongest draws for students.

On February 29, 1984, PNC suffered a loss when Robert F. Schwarz passed away following a brief illness. Following his death, the Education Building would be renamed in his honor later that October.

TECHNOLOGY

Alspaugh's foresight into the future of the economic world was not merely an unacted upon foreshadowing. By November of 1982 PNC was involved in the computer revolution. Two years prior, PNC obtained its first computer system while by the summer of 1981 it would be operating two completely different but interfaced computer systems. Students used an IBM Series 1 System while an IBM 34 served the administrative offices. There was also a computer club and 175 students in an associate's degree computer program.

The campus had already begun to use computers for tracking student records, financial accounts, security, registration and admissions, and student jobs. There was also a student chapter of the professional Data Processing Management Association which sought to inform students about jobs and establish cooperative programs with businesses to enable on-the-job experience for students. PNC's Supervisor of Academic Computing at the time, Reg Johnson, saw a need for greater computer specialization in system analysis, design, programing, and other technical aspects.

Programing students were also allowed to use computers outside of classroom hours every day from 8:30 a.m. to 11 p.m. One such student, Bette Murray of Michigan City, wisely forecast a world in which "prices will drop," and one day computers would be readily available in most businesses and homes. Murray predicted that "Robotics will also be expanding in the marketplace, and robots are just another form of computers. You see them already: automatic checkout counters in supermarkets, automatic pricing at filling stations, midnight tellers at banks, even the new programmable microwave ovens are forms of computers." Jeff Mayes, a journalist with the Westville *Indicator,* discussed the impact of computers: "Are they harmful? No one so far has found any reason to think so, and their many advantages far outweigh any fears of them taking over the world."[8] The statement would showcase how truly ahead of the curve PNC was as twenty-three months later computers and robots would provoke some fears when James Cameron introduced the world to *The Terminator.*

As an engineer located in a portion of a state whose biggest economic strength was steel production, Alspaugh was aware of the importance of the forthcoming technological innovations about to revolutionize manufacturing. Fortunately, he was not alone as Prof. Thomas R. Brady was helping lead the way in PNC's robotics teaching. Brady led the push to train students in computerized industrial production by utilizing robots in conjunction with computer-controlled tools connected through computers. The two robots had been purchased in April 1982 at a cost of $1,800 each. The computers which operated them cost $500 each. The system also used a conveyor belt system to detect faulty parts during assembly. More impressive was the fact that students who joined Brady in the program did so as volunteers, not for grades. While Brady and his five students worked with two robots, the United States was witnessing a revolution in robotics with 12,000 in use throughout the country. Brady predicted that number was just the tip of the emerging iceberg, as he believed that 100,000 would be in operation by 1986. As for PNC, Brady and his robotics students anxiously awaited the $250,000, 4,000-square-foot industrial engineering technology lab that was set to open in January of the following year. The lab would have full-scale robots along with between $500,000 and $750,000 worth of equipment.[9] The robotics lab was viewed as an investment in the future, not just for the university, but for the community. The lab was truly a sign of PNC's entry into the future of technology. The lab afforded local business and industry the opportunity to witness the work of robots on campus, as opposed to simply relying on the advice of salespersons. With these and other essential additions, in February 1995 PNC took first place out of ten schools from across the country in the two-year college division of the Construction Management Marathon Competition sponsored by the Home Builders Institute of the National Association of Home Builders.

The lab addition, however, was not enough as Alspaugh envisioned a third major building focused on technology to be added to the campus. The technology building would finally receive approval on May 20, 1992, with construction set to begin in the spring of 1993. The delay in approval caused the 1994 opening to be delayed until 1995. In addition to the 120 classrooms, laboratories, and offices, the 104,120

The Technology Building opened in the spring of 1995, providing not only needed academic space but also new laboratories and equipment to update and expand the programs in engineering, technology and construction management. Nursing facilities and laboratories were soon added, along with a learning center and other academic support services. (PNW Archives)

square foot building also featured a Computing Center, Learning Center, Printing Services, Office of Continuing Education, and 44,000 additional square feet to be utilized as needed. It would be the first major building opened since 1975.

The construction of the technology building would not go without controversy however, as Local 150 of the International Union of Operating Engineers picketed in protest of the use of some non-union subcontractors on other projects being built by the building's general contractor, Reinke Construction Corp. The picketers said their grievance was not with the University but with Reinke. Nevertheless, the protest shut down construction on the site temporarily. The building eventually opened on May 19, 1995, including within it a time capsule to be opened in 25 years.

PNC's focus on technology led to its recognition from more than just local companies debating technology integration. Many companies donated materials for the robotics labs, and others donated computers.

This parade float from 1993 features PNC's marketing slogan, "The World Changes By Degrees." A very "catchy" phrase and popular campaign, the slogan resonated with students and gained acclaim from other institutions at national conferences. (PNW Archives)

In January 1998, PNC was selected to participate in teacher.training@microsoft. The program supplied more than $11,000 worth of the latest in computer software, free of charge, to be used by students and for teacher training courses.

For the Spring semester of 1999, PNC began listing for the first time the complete class schedule on the Purdue University North Central website. Students were still required to register for classes in person, but they could now download an application for admission, navigate information on financial aid, and view course offerings.

Budgeting and Tuition

In August 1982, concerns arose when the state of Indiana faced a $77 million shortfall in state revenues for the fiscal year. Since 66 percent of PNC's $4.8 million budget came from the state in 1982-83, the issue caused concern that tuition and fees would have to be increased. Rates had already increased by 14.95 percent to $37.50 per credit hour for resident students. A further increase could cause a potential loss of students no longer able to afford the cost of attendance.

As a counter to increasing tuition costs, former Chancellor Robert Schwarz acted as Director of Development, with the primary task of raising money. At the time, only about $40,000 of the University's $5

Playing on "The World Changes By Degrees" theme, the South Shore Line, the area's commuter railroad, paid for these very popular posters that soon became collector's items. (PNW Archives)

million budget came from contributions, with the small scholarship fund relying principally on an annual sale of donated books, records, and magazines. Schwarz began promoting donations that, up to $200 for individuals or $400 if filed jointly, could qualify for Indiana tax credits. He also planned for full-time enrollment to increase because of higher unemployment in the struggling economy. Alspaugh believed that the "practical experience" of faculty who were "often leaders in business and technology," in addition to the emphasis on "practical, specialized education first," as opposed to the usual "general education first," would continue to keep the University successful.[10]

In 1985, PNC received approval for a special services government program designed to assist first-generation college students, low-income, and handicapped students. Two-thirds of the participants needed to have two of the requirements. In 1987 the program would expand with the receipt of an $85,029 federal grant from the Department of Education to fund a Student Support Services Program for high-risk students. Two years later the program received another $91,525 from the same source. In 1987, Purdue University povided a $2,500 Affirmative Action Incentive Grant for 1987-88, the only such award to a regional campus. All of these helped to promote retention.

The other method of meeting the budget was through tuition rates. When Alspaugh arrived, tuition had just been raised for resident undergraduate students by 14.8 percent to $32.45 per credit hour. In May of 1984, PNC announced a further increase of $2.75 per credit hour for in-state residents. This was a seven percent increase in tuition cost, pushing the total to $42.25 per credit hour. This coincided with a 10.5 percent budget increase to $5,587,329 for the 1984-1985 fiscal year.

In Fall of 1994, tuition for in-state undergraduates rose from $74 to $79.25 per credit hour. That summer, placement tests became required for admittance to the university. Again in the fall of 1995 tuition rose, this time from $79.25 to $83.25 for in-state undergraduate students and PNC also began charging students a $3 per credit hour technology fee that was supposed to be used to fund computers. University spokespersons announced that the increases were required because the state had failed to fully fund the six percent increase it requested from the General Assembly.

One downside of the increasing enrollment in universities, including PNC, was the continual need for tuition increases. The fears of tuition increases did not escape Alspaugh, who suggested parents begin saving for their children's future from day one. As far back as 1989, Alspaugh said it was likely college costs would increase six percent per year at residential public universities. He expected tuition to be about $19,591 per year by 2007. To prepare for this, Alspaugh and financial aid director Jerry Lewis suggested parents start college funds early to pay for children's education. Alspaugh also reminded readers that the estimates for income gaps between college graduates and non-college graduates was $600,000 to $1,000,000 over the course of an employed lifetime.

Another downside was that by 1989, PNC was in desperate need of new space to meet the surplus of enrolled students. Three buildings were simply not enough for a student population over 3,000, and ten years of steady enrollment growth that continued to trend upwards.

PROGRAM OFFERINGS

When Alspaugh arrived as vice-chancellor in 1981, PNC offered only two baccalaureate degrees. As chancellor, he began adding new programs. In October 1983, a third baccalaureate degree program, a B.A. in Elementary Education, gained approval. In 1985, PNC added a B.S. in Mechanical Engineering Technology. In November of that year PNC established a cooperative program with Valparaiso University designed to assist registered nurses. Under the program, RN's who had an Associate of Science degree in nursing from PNC were admitted to the baccalaureate degree program in nursing at Valparaiso University at the same substantially lower public tuition rate charged by PNC. The cost difference was subsidized by the state through the Public Private Partnership in Higher Education Act. In just over four years as chancellor, Alspaugh led PNC to four-year status on October 10, 1986, making it easier for the campus to add new four-year programs to its repertoire.

In December 1987, PNC created a partnership with Ancilla College of Donaldson, Indiana, that allowed students who received an Ancilla associate degree, to earn a Bachelor of Liberal Studies degree from PNC while at Ancilla College. This was yet another effort to help local and nearby communities.

The fall of 1989 saw PNC add a fifth bachelor's degree, an English major, to its growing repertoire of four-year degrees. Four years later PNC added its final four-year degree under Alspaugh, a B.S. in Biological Sciences. This gave the campus six baccalaureate and twelve associate degrees, along with six one-year certificate programs. As Alspaugh was retiring, the campus was planning to add an MBA program in the fall of 1999 in partnership with Purdue Calumet.

Aside from courses offered on campus and at its satellites, PNC also featured a very important program it thought would help the community. Beginning in 1985, PNC offered classes and degrees for inmates at the nearby Westville Correctional Center. At the time it was the only Indiana college to offer on-site programs for prisoners. The

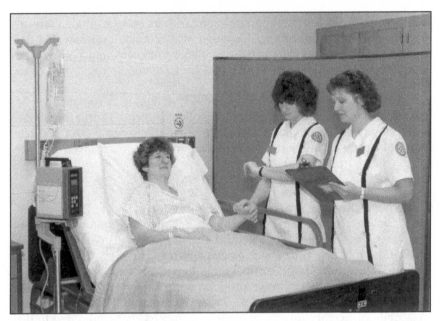

By the beginning of the 1990s, a rigorous academic program coupled with a large dose of clinical practice in hospitals and other health facilities made PNC's nursing graduates in demand throughout the region. Close ties with area hospitals led to further development of the degree program, as well as professional development opportunities for practicing professionals. (PNW Archives)

classes were taught by both full- and part-time faculty who had to pass through strict security measures to enter the prison. This program was later expanded to the prison in Michigan City with studies indicating a positive effect on the rate of recidivism; that is, prisoners attending classes while confined had a lower rate of re-incarceration once released than did those who did not enroll in classes while confined. Data indicated then that 82 percent of offenders who were released were back in prison within five years. College programs reduced that rate to about 15 percent, saving lives and saving taxpayer money. During the first 15 years of the PNC program it enrolled approximately 500 inmates. Less than a dozen returned to prison, a rate of under than three percent.

Finally, in 1985 PNC granted Michigan City businessman John Garrettson the Doctor of Laws, its first honorary degree.

Halloween was a special occasion for children on the PNC campus. In this 1991 photograph, the children and staff in the campus child care facility are dressed for their Halloween party. (PNW Archives)

COMMUNITY EVENTS

Pursuing Alspaugh's vision of the Land Grant mission, PNC hosted many campus and community events, including regular blood drives. Some of the most notable include the following:

- February 9, 1983 — hosting a farming course concerning the Payment in Kind program which paid farmers with corn or wheat instead of dollars if they participated in the 1983 Feed Grain Program sponsored by the U.S. Department of Agriculture. The meeting featured a closed-circuit television hook up with the main Purdue Campus.

- February 1983 — A regional meeting of the Indiana Council of Teachers of Mathematics, coordinated by PNC assistant professor of mathematics, Michael A. Kasper.

- March 21, 1983 — A Nursing Career Day attracted as many as 30 health care agencies from across the U.S.

- Hosting annual Northwestern Indiana Science and Engineering Fairs.

- April 9, 1983 — A Women's Conference featuring prominent participants including Virginia Dill McCarthy, the former U.S. attorney for Indiana's Southern District, and U.S. Representative Katie Hall, Indiana's first African-American female elected to Congress.

- April 20, 1983 — An exhibit of English antiques and fragments dating as far back as the 17th century hosted in the PNC library.

- October 14, 1983 — A workshop on "Exporting for Profit: The Why's and How's of Selling Overseas."

- October 15, 1983 — An exhibit featuring computers for the home and business, word processors, and robotics.

- November 1983 — The beginning of a conference series, fund by a $5,060 grant, featuring "The Afro-American Family in the Mid-1980s," "Hispanic-American: Status and Identity in the United States," and "The New Americans: Southeast Asian Immigrants."

- 1985 — In this and subsequent years, PNC hosted "Super Saturday," a program designed for intelligent children in kindergarten through 10th grade, with IQ's above 115 that were referred from their teachers.

- 1988 — A year-long celebration of women, titled "Women on the Move," the intent of which was to create a greater awareness of the opportunities available to women at PNC.

- March 22, 1988 — A forum "Racism on Campus: Toward an Agenda for Action," a national videoconference organized by Governors State University and the Johnson Foundation. The program highlighted preventative measures to end racial incidents on campuses.

- On April 15, 1988 — A conference on "Productivity and Quality of Work Life" to help local employers improve productivity.

- November 1988 — A series of educational and informative programs on AIDS during AIDS Awareness Week.

- August 28, 1989 — The "Chancellor's Series" began, a

performing arts and lecture series featuring guest speakers and performers from drama, politics, motivation, education, history, and music.

- October 1989 — A"Women in Supervision" seminar offered insights into the management of people at work.

NOTABLE FACULTY ACHIEVEMENTS

Under Chancellor Alspaugh's leadership, faculty began to receive encouragement and support for research activities. In the fall on 1982, Roger C. Schlobin, an Associate Professor of English who was recognized as one of the foremost fantasy scholars, published his edited *The Aestethics of Fantasy Literature and Art.* Two years later he followed with authorship of *Urania's Daughters: A Checklist of Women Science-Fiction Writers 1682-1982.* In September 1983, history Prof. Howard Jablon published *Crossroads of Decision: The State Department and Foreign Policy, 1933-37,* the first major critical publication about the U.S. State Department's New Deal diplomacy. The following month Schlobin published *Word Choice: An Advanced Guide to Selecting a CP/M Processor and a Microcomputer for Home, University and Business,* designed to assist computer purchasers in selecting microcomputers. In 1998, part-time instructor Rod Rolston capitalized on his experience in the prison education program with *Vignettes from a Prison Educator,* intended for criminal justice students.

SPORTS AND OTHER COMPETITIONS

Because PNC was a commuter campus, sports were not a prevalent part of its early history, yet there were some notable events. The first Purdue North Central Softball Tournament took place in 1981 and the following year PNC added women's intercollegiate volleyball and hosted what became an annual basketball tournament. Under Alspaugh, PNC built a new baseball field and joined the National Association of Intercollegiate Athletics (NAIA) IN 1999.

ALSPAUGH'S LEGACY

In November 1996, Purdue made an exception to its retirement policy by allowing Chancellor Alspaugh to delay his retirement for two years. This was the first time an exception had been made to the 1978 retirement clause requiring administrators with the rank of dean and above to retire from those positions at age 65. Alspaugh's success and vision was considered too valuable to lose. Under his tenure as Chancel-

Although developing its own athletic teams, throughout the Alspaugh years the PNC community maintained close ties to the "Boilermaker" athletic teams. Frequent visits to the area by the Purdue University musical organizations, speakers, and the "Boilermaker Special" helped sustain that relationship. (PNW Archives)

lor of PNC, enrollment increased by 30 percent and credit hours increased by 45 percent. He had also added multiple two- and four-year degree programs. Alspaugh's vision was not complete as he still was requesting a fourth major building for multipurpose activities such as the inclusion of a gymnasium and assembly hall. This fourth building was in conflict with a request submitted for a different and separate fourth building that would house liberal-arts activities to undergo construction in 1999.

Alspaugh, who was supposed to retire in 1996, carried on into 1999 after his previous extension. He was scheduled to retire on July 1, 1999, and a search for a replacement chancellor ensued. With four finalists set to interview that spring, none were selected, and once again Alspaugh remained. As retirement loomed, Alspaugh reflected on the last 18 years, "I think the best thing about this job is the kind of experiences you have meeting people and perhaps changing their lives forever."[11] By November of 1999, a successor would finally be chosen as chancellor, James B. Dworkin. Alspaugh finally retired as both PNC and the world entered a new millennium.

Alspaugh also began to receive honors for his work at PNC, including Indiana's highest honor, the Sagamore of the Wabash awarded by Governor Frank O'Bannon. The word Sagamore was said to have meant, "someone of great wisdom."

Though this is a history of the University, and not the man, the Purdue North Central campus was truly indebted to Dale Alspaugh. Eighteen years previous when Alspaugh arrived at PNC, the campus was a place that some referred to as "Pretty Near College," and "a high school where you can smoke." One student had even been overheard by Schwarz as saying "I'm not going to college. I'm going to Purdue North Central."[12] Alspaugh's vision and leadership helped to shift the view of PNC into a much more respectable institution. It was the groundwork, the engineering, of Dale Alspaugh that allowed PNC's success.

Dale W. Alspaugh passed away July 1, 2004 at just 72 years of age. Forty of Alspaugh's 72 years were spent within the Purdue system where he began as a graduate student in 1959, earning two masters degrees and a doctorate. Having had a goal to enter the private sector, he instead remained at Purdue West Lafayette where he became an Assistant Professor in 1964 and Associate Professor in 1968, instructing potential future astronauts in aeronautics, astronautics and engineering. As if training astronauts was not enough, Alspaugh took on his next challenge in 1981 when he became the vice-chancellor of Purdue North Central, a small campus surrounded by farmlands. The next year he became acting chancellor before being named chancellor in 1984. PNC's enrollment increased by 831 during Alspaugh's tenure, while credit hours expanded by over 10,000. Under Alspaugh, PNC became a four-year institution, added four new bacccalaureate degrees, four associate degrees, several professional certificate programs, and an MBA was ready to begin operation at the time of his retirement. Most importantly, Alspaugh helped bring education to the local communities he served. Be it the successes of adding students, buildings, or technology in an ever-changing world, nothing truer could be said of Dale Alspaugh than the words spoken by PNC's then Vice-Chancellor for Academic Affairs Edward Bednar — "he bled black and old gold."[13]

[1] "English Oxford Living Dictionaries," https://en.oxforddictionaries.com/definition/engineer.

[2] The B.S. in supervision was approved May 1980, while the Bachelor of Liberal Studies degree was approved in September 1981 following Alspaugh's arrival.

[3] This and other data in this article comes from PNC memoranda and reports in the PNW Archives.

[4] Dale Alspaugh, "Up to You," *Indicator*, Nov. 4, 1982.

[5] Ibid.; Dale Alspaugh, "Indiana Facing 'Brain Drain' Crisis," *News-Dispatch*, Oct. 1, 1983.

[6] Dale W. Alspaugh, "It's Not Too Late to Continue Your Education," *News-Dispatch*, Jan. 13, 1984.

[7] Dale Alspaugh, "Purdue University North Central Waging Campaign to Raise $2 Million." *News-Dispatch*, Oct. 7, 1992.

[8] "Computers in Classes, Offices, Club at PNC," *Indicator*, Nov. 25, 1982.

[9] "PNC Professor, Students Work on Computerized Production Line," *Herald-Argus*, Feb. 27, 1984.

[10] "State Revenue Shortfall Likely to Affect PNC," *News-Dispatch*, Aug. 5, 1982.

[11] "A Believer in Education," *Times*, June 28, 1999.

[12] "PNC Chancellor Alspaugh to Retire," *Harold-Argus*, March 25, 1999.

[13] "The State's Highest Honor," *News-Dispatch*, May 7, 1999.

THE DWORKIN YEARS: 2000-2015

Joshua Koepke

Chancellor James B. Dworkin took the podium on May 16, 2016, for his final commencement address to the Purdue North Central graduating class, reflecting on one of his achievements during his sixteen years as the head of the campus:

> We are very happy to have you join us at this momentous occasion. As I told you earlier, we are really making history here tonight, graduates and guests, you should be very proud of the fact that you are experiencing the very first commencement — and actually the very first event in the James B. Dworkin Student Services and Activities Complex. And I can't really express in words how thrilled I am that our graduates can now receive their degrees on the campus that they actually earned their degrees, pretty cool.[1]

Not mentioned in this quote were the other significant changes that happened under his time as the head of Purdue North Central. By the end of Dworkin's tenure, not only had he assisted in creating a new building for the campus, but had helped to fundamentally shift the trajectory of the institution and ultimately guided the institution to its end. PNC's last day of existence was also the last day Dworkin's chancellorship — June 30, 2016. Effective the following day, the newly founded Purdue University Northwest became official with a merger between two regional campuses in the Purdue University system, Purdue North Central and Purdue Calumet. The Dworkin administration transitioned Purdue North Central in several ways: the institution took a very active and central role in community involvement, PNC changed from primarily an associate's degree granting institution to a bachelor's degree granting campus, the core demographic of the PNC student morphed from previous standards, and the physical infrastructure of the campus expanded.

The search for the successor to Chancellor Alspaugh was a long process, with Dworkin not being on the initial list of candidates. Purdue President Steven C. Beering, having rejected the two finalists from the initial nationwide search, further extended the retiring Alspaugh's already prolonged contract.[2] The fall semester of 1999

James B. Dworkin arrived from the Krannert School of Management in West Lafayette where he had been since 1976 to assume the position of PNC chancellor in January 2000. (PNW Archives)

brought phone calls from the Vice President for Academic Affairs, Robert Ringel, and President Beering to the then Associate Dean of the Krannert School of Management, James Dworkin. Dworkin earned his bachelor's and master's degrees from the University of Cincinnati and his Ph. D. from the University of Minnesota. He specialized in negotiations and conflict resolution, with special interest in Major League Baseball, writing two books on conflict resolution in the MLB.[3] Singled out for the interview process, Dworkin gained the job and officially started on January 1, 2000.[4] Dworkin's appointment as chancellor was unusual, for chancellors commonly come from administrative positions directly under the current chancellor – say a provost or vice chancellor. Dworkin himself aptly used a baseball metaphor to compare himself becoming chancellor versus the norm, saying that baseball players usually do not rise from single-A leagues or directly from college to the major leagues; it is usually a more methodical rise through the ranks of the various minor leagues.[5] Regardless, Dworkin started in the position of PNC Chancellor and already had plans for the future of the institution.

INCREASING COMMUNITY INVOLVEMENT

An important mark for the campus during this time period was the continued, and increased presence of the institution in the greater community. This involvement was even a featured goal of the 2008-2014 strategic plan.[6] Individually, numerous professors and administrative staff gained or maintained prestigious and influential positions on local government and non-government organizations. For example Jeff Jones, at the time the Director of Enrollment and Marketing, was appointed to the Michigan City Sanitation District Board by the Mayor of Michigan City, Sheila Brillson. While doing this, Jones also served as "a member of the board of the Boys and Girls Club of Michigan City, vice chairman of the Michigan City Area Chamber of Commerce and past chairman of the LaPorte Regional Health System."[7] Prof. Beryle Burgwald served on the Michigan City Area Schools Board of Trustees beginning in 2007, and had previously served on the Michigan City Council for sixteen years.[8] Dr. Cynthia Roberts was a part of the Michigan City Area Chamber of Commerce starting in 2014.[9] The list could go on for quite a while, clearly many PNC staff worked with the public.

Additionally, Dworkin himself was heavily involved in community affairs, and was responsible for some of the institution's community programs. He focused on his background in business and labor relations to join or head several organizations focused on economic development, and used his position as chancellor to further educational initiatives. Because he was chancellor, Dworkin was invited to join the then named Northwest Indiana Quality of Life Council. This organization pushed for economic development and educational advancements for the region, as well as maintaining the highest possible standard of living for the area's residents. He was also invited to join the LaPorte County United Way by its then chairwoman, an organization in which he eventually became chairman. He served until his term limit, then joined the Porter County United Way.[10] PNC as an institution was recognized by the LaPorte United Way as the 2008 Cornerstone Award Organization for its contributions. As of 2018, Dworkin still worked for the state division of United Way, and summarized his involvement: "My whole life I've thought that, from those people who much is given, we ought to give a lot back, so I really believed in the United Way."[11]

Dworkin also established the College Bound Program for PNC. Entirely funded through private donations, many of which originated from local businesses, the College Bound Program focused on getting low-income, first-time college students, and minorities into PNC by providing scholarships to qualifying students. Starting with an initial class of 25 seventh graders in Michigan City, it expanded rapidly, giving college

A unique competition made possible by the Development Office was the regional "Business Plan Competition" sponsored jointly by PNC and the Purdue-Calumet campus. The three top finishers received cash prizes to assist them in developing their business idea. Here Chancellor Dworkin and Purdue Calumet Vice Chancellor for Academic Affairs Nabil Ibrahim present the winning check for $25,000 to Brogan Pharmaceuticals. (PNW Archives)

opportunities to 518 students in Michigan City, Portage, and LaPorte schools by October of 2014.[12] In addition, Dworkin created the LaPorte County Economic Development Organization, which combined the shared interests between the cities of Michigan City and LaPorte to stop competing with each other and work together to attract jobs, development, and tourism.[13] Under Chancellor Dworkin, PNC also partnered with the cities of LaPorte and Michigan City to establish a bus line that ran between the three destinations; "Ever since I arrived here, I have been thinking about having some sort of commuter system to and from areas like LaPorte and Michigan City. This would help those who have trouble finding a way to get out here to get an education," said

Shakespeare's Garden, adjacent to Bard's Pond, was a popular site for relaxation and meditation amid nature, as well as a location for frequent lectures and class meetings. (PNW Archives)

Dworkin.[14] His idea, named the Transit Triangle, became a reality on February 2, 2015, with $20,000 donations from the three member destinations and a large federal grant.[15] Finally, Dworkin originated the idea to join together the Sinai Forum and PNC.[16] The Sinai Forum was an association which paid speakers to come to Northwest Indiana to give lectures to the public. The Forum has attracted such names as former Head of the Federal Bureau of Investigation James Comey and famed journalist Bob Woodward throughout its existence. Interesting and popular speakers do not come cheap though, as the Forum cited higher speaker fees as a reason for the partnership, which was finalized in 2006.[17] Since taking control in 2000, Dworkin's major focus was creating a more involved approach in the community.

Although not meant to explain the complete reasons behind such community involvement, there existed a motivating reason for PNC's tenure-track professors to be involved in the community. A key portion of the official guidelines of PNC to grant tenure to tenure-track professors was "excellence in engagement." This consisted of numerous activities including: "Consultation to outside agencies and institutions," and, "Participation in community development activities at the local, regional, and state levels."[18] Clearly, tenure and promotion criteria looked favorably on community involvement. Additionally, from an institutional standpoint, community participation was highly valued. One of the requirements when PNC was transitioned from an associate's degree granting status by the Indiana Commission for Higher Education (ICHE) to a bachelor's degree granting university status, was an increased focus by the university in community developments:

> The Indiana Commission for Higher Education provides a framework for discovery at regional campuses: "All four-year public campuses will be involved in applied research projects and activities that support local and regional economic development and address the needs of business and industry."[19]

This was also noted on the official PNC petition for academic autonomy finished on August 16, 2005. It clearly stated as the sixth and final "additional points that support this petition for campus academic autonomy" that: "Purdue University North Central has taken a leading position in economic development and other engagement activities in the area it serves and has been recognized for this leadership by area chambers of commerce, economic development offices, and businesses and governmental agencies."[20] It is important to note that Chancellor Dworkin indicated that no such idea was present or influential, but the report was created by PNC administrators for ICHE officials.[21]

A positive result of these community initiatives was, as Dr. Cynthia Roberts, the former Dean of the School of Business at PNC stated, that being a part of community organizations was good publicly for PNC. It not only exposed the public to the PNC name, but did so in a positive light. In addition, such involvement could be a strategic recruitment tool for attracting students to the institution.[22]

THE DEVELOPMENT OF ACADEMIC PROGRAMS

Under Chancellor Dworkin, Purdue North Central continued its transition from an associate's degree granting institution to a baccalaureate granting university, which led to changes in available programs. When Dworkin started in January of 2000, there were twelve associate, six baccalaureate, and one master degrees available to students. It was one of his goals when taking over to create more bachelor degree options.[23] Subsequently, the campus added baccalaureate programs in nursing, business, engineering, history, psychology, human resources, early childhood education, behavioral sciences, computer information services, and social work.[24] A degree in health studies in 2013 was the last baccalaureate degree approved during the Dworkin era, bringing the total number to 24.[25]

The secret to expanding the degree offerings, and so rapidly, was the granting of academic autonomy for the campus. The idea for autonomy was not a new one. As early as 1994, there was significant correspondence between the Higher Learning Commission of the North Central Association of Colleges and Schools and PNC regarding the need for autonomy. One report candidly stated:

> The 1994 team expressed concern with the future of the relationship between Purdue North Central and the home campus of Purdue University, especially as it relates to strategic planning. Since that time, the leaders of both campuses have been working toward a plan for the autonomy of the Purdue North Central campus.[26]

Chancellor Dworkin did provide immediate support for the cause and provided a general plan to move toward academic autonomy. On December 18, 2000, Purdue President Martin Jischke approved this plan, although it would not be until February 6, 2006 that PNC would actually gain autonomy.[27] Until the granting of academic autonomy in 2006, the main campus in West Lafayette exercised significant oversight of PNC. The various department heads on the main campus had final authority over any changes to graduation requirements, course changes, and degrees offered. This oversight function slowed changes in degree programs dramatically. But not only did the main campus have oversight of degrees, they also held significant roles in many other important areas. As Dworkin explained in 2006, "full academic autonomy gives PNC greater flexibility, not only in developing its own curriculum, but also in hiring faculty, setting academic schedules, and in admissions and graduation requirements."[28] Without autonomy, other changes would not have been able to take place. Such as the revisions to PNC general education core classes in 2012 which allowed for a universal 30-credit hour general education core regardless of major. This permitted students to transfer more credit hours if they switched majors. During the same negotiations, the total number of credit hours for most degrees went to a standardized 120 credit hours; previously some degrees had as many as 129 credit hours.[29] Shortly after autonomy, PNC changed its overall academic structure from "divisions" to "colleges," which would not have been possible without autonomy. For these reasons, academic autonomy was essential to the growth of PNC, as

Top: Prof. Tantatape Brahmasrene (fourth from left) was PNC's first Fulbright Fellow. Here he is pictured with students on a travel-study trip to his native Thailand in 2004. (PNW Archives) Bottom: Students and community people in Prof. James Pula's course on the Civil War gather around one of the monuments at the Gettysburg National Military Park. (James S. Pula)

Left: Prof. Alain Togbe received his doctorate from Laval University in Québec, Canada. He is an acknowledged international expert in algebraic number theory and Diophantine equations. Right: Prof. Silvia G. Dapía is an internationally recognized literary scholar who earned her doctorate at the University of Cologne in Germany. In 2006 she became the founding Dean of the College of Liberal Arts and the first female appointed to a senior leadership position in PNC history. (PNW Archives)

Prof. David J. Feikes, seen here working with local school children, obtained funding from the National Science Foundation to develop a better way of teaching mathematics in elementary schools. (PNW Archives)

Prof. James Pula, a specialist in immigration and 19th century U.S. history holds honors including the Officers' Cross of the Order of Merit from the Republic of Poland. (PNW Archives)

Prof. Sharron Jenkins, the author of the acclaimed African American Health Disparities, *developed an innovative distance learning course on Aids and the HIV virus. (PNW Archives)*

Prof. Richard Hengst, a paleobiologist, each year took students on his expeditions to Utah to dig for dinosaur bones. With him in 2006 were (form left) Jim Early, Kristin Pairitz, Michael Crowley, Dr. Hengst, John Bird, Cameron Kelly-Jones, Lara Uriadko, Jonathan De La Cruz and Adrian Miramontes. (PNW Archives)

In keeping with PNC's emphasis on engagement, Prof. Purna Das explains a physics experiment to sixth graders from the Edgewood School. A professor of physics, he received grants from the National Science Foundation for his research on small solid state particles and solid surfaces, linear and nonlinear spectroscopic properties of adsorbates near small particles and solid surfaces, and the physics of nanoparticles and nano-scale structures. (PNW Archives)

Prof. Maria Ofelia Ziegenfus, a native of Peru, directed the language lab with creative ideas and enthusiasm. She also took students to study in Peru. (PNW Archives)

Prof. Diane Maletta served as editor of the Indiana Reading Journal, a publication of the Indiana State Reading Association. (PNW Archives)

Prof. Michael Connolly was an editor of Praeger Publishing's Series on American Political Culture. (PNW Archives)

Prof. Keith Schwingendorf obtained over $1 million in grants and sponsored research funding. (PNW Archives)

Prof. Drew Weiss developed PNC's innovative and highly successful MBA program. (PNW Archives)

Dworkin stated, "I put Feb. 3, 2006, right up there with the dates 1946, when the courses were allowed to be held in different regions of the state and with 1967 when we opened PNC."[30]

Why the push for bachelor degree options, and why under Dworkin? The main answer lay with the creation of Ivy Tech Community College. The year 1999 was an eventful year for the Northwest Indiana college scene. Not only was Dworkin hired at PNC, but the Indiana legislature created the statewide Ivy Tech Community College system as an associate's degree granting college from what had to that point been a largely vocational school. As journalist Erik Lords explained, up until that point associate degrees were primarily granted by four-year institutions: "Three decades ago, when many states were erecting two-year colleges as quickly as possible, Indiana took a different approach: It chose to have the regional campuses of Purdue and Indiana Universities generate the bulk of its associate degrees. That decision has not produced the best results."[31]

The idea was to slowly transition associate degrees from other institutions and concentrate them into Ivy Tech. The creation of this new community college model was completed in the fall of 2005 when Indiana Governor Joe Kernan officially granted Ivy Tech sole ownership of associate-level programs and transitioned all of its 23 locations to associate degree granting institutions.[32] At this point, the state mandated that PNC, along with all other state-supported campuses, would have to relinquish their associate degree programs to Ivy Tech so as to avoid wasting resources though competition. Without moving to baccalaureate degrees, PNC would have faced steep enrollment losses as its two-year progms were phased out.[33]

When Dworkin took over in 2000 PNC had only six baccalaureate degrees along with its twelve associate degrees.[34] Even more discerning was the number of students enrolled in bachelor degrees versus associate degrees at the time. "Purdue University North Central: Focused Visit Report 2003," an internal report, showed that in 2000 only 24 percent of campus enrollment was in bacccalaureate programs.[35] That year 31.6 percent of degrees offered were bachelor degrees — one master's, six baccalaureates, and twelve associates.

The struggle of adding new degree options did not start with Dworkin, one of Alspaugh's regrets when he retired was not being able to get more options for students.[36] Although the last years of Alspaugh's term did see a slight improvement in the percent of students in bachelor degrees, from 20 percent in 1994 to 22 percent in 1999. The granting of autonomy was a key step to the new surge of degree options. By the end of Dworkin's era, serious gains were made in adding baccalaureate degrees. For example, in 2000 there were 141 students graduating with baccalaureate degrees versus 237 with associate degrees. In May 2016, PNC's last graduation ceremony, there were 501 baccalaureates awarded and only 36 associate degrees.[37]

Rather than having to compete against Ivy Tech at the associate degree level, PNC expanded baccalaureate degrees and partnered with Ivy Tech to attract more students to its programs through articulation agreements that standardized acceptance of transfer credits to provide students with a smooth transition from Ivy Tech to pursue baccalaureate degrees at Purdue North Central.[38] Although this strategy placed PNC into competition against other regional four-year universities (Valparaiso University, Indiana University Northwest, Indiana University South Bend, and Purdue University Calumet), this transition was essential for PNC's survival because of the loss of its two-year programs. Valparaiso University would now prove a more direct competitor, but PNC still provided a different fundamental product as a public university with an internationally recognized name and a much lower cost of attendance.

ENROLLMENT GROWTH

During the Dworkin era, overall student demographics changed significantly with several noteworthy shifts in enrollment statistics. The most obvious was total enrollment, noted on Table 1, which jumped from 3,459 students in the fall 2000 semester to 6,158 in the fall of 2015, PNC's last fall semester.[39]

TABLE 1: FALL ENROLLMENTS

Year	Total	Core	Dual*	Year	Total	Core	Dual
2000	3,459			2008	4,241		
2001	3,493			2009	4,463		
2002	3,657			2010	4,614	3,989	625
2003	3,469			2011	5,279	3,635	1,644
2004	3,441			2012	6,048	3,573	2,475
2005	3,520			2013	6,102	3,580	2,522
2006	3,724			2014	6,177	3,287	2,890
2007	3,904			2015	6,158	3,059	2,937

*Dual refers to the concurrent enrollment program for students in high schools.

Table 1 was compiled through a combination of PNC press releases and local newspaper articles on enrollment with enrollment numbers. These two sources were generally in agreement as comparing press releases to corresponding articles show marked similarities on wording between the two sources. The overall increase appears substantial, but the "total enrollment" figure itself must be explained to reach a true understanding. Total enrollment refers to every individual currently registered for classes that would potentially receive PNC credit. This notably includes dual credit high school students who never actually step foot on the campus and are not taught by PNC professors. As noted in the table, this category exploded between 2010 and 2015. An examination of sources both in the PNW archive and externally show a corresponding lack of clarification of the "total enrollment" figure to include a separate high school and core enrollment breakdown, on both third party newspaper clippings and PNC press releases, until 2010. But Table 2 provides an enrollment breakdown from PNW's "Fact Book" that shows that PNC internally recorded the category of "High School Students" as early as Fall 2008.[40]

TABLE 2: FALL ENROLLMENTS FROM "FACT BOOK"

Year	Total	Headcount Core	Dual	Year	Percent of Total Core	Dual
2008	4,235	3,926	309	2008	92.7	7.3
2009	4,463	3,952	511	2009	88.6	11.4
2010	4,614	3,972	642	2010	86.1	13.9
2011	5,279	3,621	1,658	2011	68.6	31.4
2012	6.048	3,573	2,475	2012	59.1	40.9
2013	6,102	3,590	2,522	2013	58.7	41.3
2014	6,177	3,287	2,890	2014	53.2	46.8
2015	6,158	3,221	2,560	2015	52.3	47.7

There exist small differences between the figures in Table 1 and Table 2. These numeric differences are not large, but do raise questions since PNC press releases are official documents, like the "Fact Book," and thus should not differ. One possible explanation would be the date of compilation of the statistics, which were noted in the newspaper articles/press releases as early in the fall semester (typically in late August or early September) whereas the "Fact Book" did not mention at what point in the semester the data was from. As the tables show, the most substantial growth in high school enrollment appeared after 2010, but high school programs were not new, they originated before Dworkin became chancellor. From the fall 2008 semester, which saw 309 in the dual credit/concurrent enrollment programs, to the fall 2015 semester's 2,937, dual enrollment experienced a 850.5 percent increase.[41] This not only made the overall enrollment figure deceptive, but in the long run had a detrimental affect on the budget and core enrollments. Since dual enrollment students paid only a few dollars per credit hour, the campus lost that potential tuition. Further, since high school students were receiving credit for freshman-level courses such as English, history, and mathematics, enrollment in those on-campus courses began to decline since many incoming students had already earned credit for them.[42]

The PNC 2011 "Higher Learning Commission Self-Study," summarized the major causes of enrollment growth from the late 2000s to 2011: "Overall enrollment has increased. However, most of the enrollment increase has been in dual credit and prison programs."[43] High school programs had such a massive effect on total enrollment that even when the prison program effectively ended at PNC in 2012 due to state funding cuts to educational grants to felons, fall 2012 total enrollment still managed to increase by some 14.56 percent.[44] Even without dedicated core enrollment figures for the earlier 2000s, core enrollment still managed to increase to a high of 3,989 in 2010, higher than the total enrollment of 3,459 in the fall of 2000. One factor could be the increase in the number of baccalaureate degree programs, which Dworkin argued back in 2005 was raising enrollment numbers, and/or the increases could be partially a result of the rough economic situation of the Great Recession which Robert Rich, an Assistant Vice President at the Federal Reserve Bank of New York, stated was worse from about 2007 to 2009, although the slow recovery lasted several years beyond that.[45] Support for the latter came from neighboring universities which also recorded increased enrollment during this time. For example, at Indiana University Northwest "Diane Hodges, vice chancellor for student affairs, said in [a] release that the economic recession likely played a large part in the increased enrollment."[46] Overall, total enrollment during Dworkin's tenure saw tremendous growth thanks largely to advances in the realm of high school students, with an otherwise fairly consistent core enrollment, influenced by the increasing degree offerings and the economic situation.

Not only did the total number of students change under Dworkin, but the type of student attending PNC also shifted during this time. There was a substantial increase in the percentage of full-time students. The fall 2000 semester recorded 53.6 percent of the total students as full-time, whereas Dworkin's last fall semester in 2015 had 75 percent of core students as full-time. It is important to note that total students included the category of high school students in 2000, while the 2015 figure did not; although the number of individuals in this category was vastly lower in the early 2000's. This increase in fulltime students was key in growing the number of credit hours per student from 9.66 in the fall of 2000 to 12.16 in the fall of 2015.[47]

Moving students to full-time status was also promoted because it might help correct the exceptionally low graduation rate. By encouraging students to take more classes they would presumably graduate faster. Also, the state funding formula had changed from enrollment numbers to include the number of completed credit hours as a major basis for state aid. Thus, a continued low completion rate would adversely effect the amount of state funding the campus received. As argued in the "Higher Learning Commission Self-Study: 2011":

> The State of Indiana is [*sic*] increasingly based funding upon performance, as measured by successfully completed credit hours, change in the number of degrees, change in on-time graduation rate and low income degree incentive. PNC has seen improving performance on these measures, which would result in a total percentage change of 2011 to 2013 of 2.8%, if the Indiana General Assembly implements ICHE recommendations.[48]

Because of these benefits, PNC instituted a tuition discount program that began in the fall of 2014. This program gave students a ten percent discount for every credit hour after twelve. It incentivized students to take more classes to keep students on track to graduate in four years.[49] This program showed some initial benefits, as students collectively saved over $100,000 on an extra 4,523 credit hours during its first semester.[50] However, during these years about half of the incoming freshmen did not meet the minimum standard for admission, and with the state prohibiting regional campuses from offering remedial courses it is not altogether clear that this initiative succeeded as the retention rate from the freshman to sophomore levels continued to hover around only fifty percent.[51]

The graduation rate was a concern for the chancellor and other top Purdue officials during the first sixteen years of the new millennium. PNC's six-year graduation rate in 1999 was only twelve percent.[52] By 2014, the six year graduation rate was up to 37.4 percent, most likely due to the traditionally higher retention rates of full-time versus part-time students.[53] Despite these gains, criticism of PNC's graduation rate was noticeable throughout Dworkin's tenure. In 2012 when then-Governor Mitch Daniels came to PNC, he was vocal in his thoughts on PNC graduation numbers, noting that out of the approximately 100 students in the room "97 of you will not finish on time, 86 of you won't finish at all. That's unacceptable."[54]

In an attempt to address this problem, Dworkin increased the number of baccalaureate options, promoted the College Bound program that provided funds for poor and underprivileged college students, and created new incentives to attract former students back to PNC to finish their degrees. Among the latter was a tuition discount program started in 2015 to help pay for tuition of former students who left in good-academic standing.[55] As Chancellor Dworkin mentioned in an interview in 2018, regional campuses virtually always have lagging graduation metrics, "because of the nature of the customer that you have."[56] Nevertheless, a study by the *The Fiscal Times* in May 2012 ranked PNC among the eleven worst performing regional campuses in the country.[57]

CAMPUS INFRASTRUCTURE

Finally, several aspects of the infrastructure of the physical campus and surrounding area significantly changed under the direction of Chancellor Dworkin. Through his sixteen and a half years at the helm, noteworthy renovations came from changes to existing buildings and through the construction of new buildings. Physical expansion and renovation of the campus appeared a major goal for Dworkin from his start, as *Post Tribune* reporter Stan Maddux reported just a few weeks into Dworkin's tenure that he planned on adding three new buildings (a theatre/auditorium building, a fourth classroom building, and a student-focused multipurpose building) and two major updates to existing buildings (updating the ground floor and first floor of the Library Student Faculty Building and finishing the third floor of the Technology Building).[58] Although a bit ambitious with his initial goals, his infrastructure endeavors contributed some of the most important overall strategies that he developed.

To begin with, Dworkin officially opened the Indiana Dunes Research Station. Although Chancellor Alspaugh originally planned and found the money to fund the renovations to create the station, it was under Dworkin that the station officially opened for research purposes. Updating an older house in the Indiana Dunes, the new research station included specialized equipment for biological research. Opening in July of 2000, this station provided the "campus's first off-site research base."[59] It also promoted an appreciation for scientific research and scholarship.

Chancellor Dworkin also oversaw the final finishes to the Technology Building. Started under the previous administration, the third floor opened for the fall 2000 semester included 17,000 square feet of labs, classrooms, and offices. The finished product cost $3.6 million, but netted a modern space for students and expanded room for some degree programs.[60]

The other major remodel of an existing building was the Library Student Faculty Building. Again originally under a plan devised by

In July 2000, PNC leased from the National Park Service a 1,000 square foot facility for use as a Biology Field Station. Once suitably renovated, it offered students and faculty opportunities to conduct research in the rich natural surroundings. The unique opportunity to study fresh-water issues drew scholars from other universities who stayed in the Field Station's overnight accommodations during the summer to conduct their own studies. (PNW Archives)

Chancellor Alspaugh, Dworkin oversaw major changes to the ground and first floors of LSF. One of Dworkin's major goals when coming to PNC was to create a more student centered environment, "I want this to be a student-friendly facility," he said. This would be one of the first major ways to achieve that objective. PNC's "Institutional Self-Study" in 2001 described the endeavor as, "The conversion of the ground and first floors of the LSF Building to a student union facility."[61] The changes were very transformative, including a weight room, workout room, lounges, a larger bookstore, and several rooms for student organizations with offices for coaches on the ground floor. The first floor added a computer lab for students, a full service cafeteria with a large seating area, and even created the new position of head chief, which was first occupied by Keith Peffers. The Cafeteria was the last to be remod-

In December 2000 PNC opened its Valparaiso Academic Center providing 10,000 square feet of classrooms, conference rooms and an executive education seminar room. Remodeled as a corporate training center with state-of-the-art technology and satellite capability, "the Vac" became the center of PNC's continuing education and professional development engagement activities. (PNW Archives)

eled, opening February 28, 2006.[62] The LSF remodel was important because it added features that never existed on campus before, namely the weight room and a full-fledged cafeteria, as well as greatly expanding other facilities. The student-friendly approach also allowed a space for students to relax in between classes, something that had been scarce before the remodeling.

The era of expansion continued with the creation of a PNC presence in the key town of Valparaiso, Indiana. PNC held remote classes in local areas for many years before Dworkin became chancellor, with these localized classes having two major advantages: they reduced the class load on the main campus, thus allowing for additional course offerings and student enrollment without having to build additional physical infrastructure in Westville; and allowed potential students to commute less by staying within their own community. The Valparaiso expansion was unique because previous local PNC classes were shared spaces within a community in existing buildings (namely local schools) that did not allow PNC sole access to the location. The initial Valparaiso expansion, originally named the Valparaiso Academic Center, gave

PNC complete control of 10,000 square feet of space for a ten year contract worth $1.25 million. It included eight classrooms, eight offices, a lecture hall, conference room, and recreation area.[63] Changes took place in 2006 with the addition of another building (dividing undergrad and graduate students by building), and changing the name of the now budding local campus to Purdue University North Central – Porter County.[64] In 2007 the owner of the buildings that PNC leased, renowned local real estate entrepreneur Harley Snyder, donated the buildings to PNC, making it the largest gift received in its history.[65] Expansion continued in 2009 with the Board of Works and Safety for Valparaiso leasing a parking lot – formerly used by Ivy Tech – for the sum of one dollar per year for the next 99 years. The future of the site looked promising in 2009, having a substantial enrollment increase from 200 at the start of operations to around a 1,000 in 2009, with Vice Chancellor Bill Back projecting enrollment to increase to at least 2,000 students by 2014.[66] Unfortunately enrollment dropped at the Valparaiso campus in the final years of PNC, and it ceased to exist along with the institution of PNC after the spring semester of 2016.[67]

The Valparaiso expansion was an interesting experiment in an area convenient for students attending a commuter campus. The Valparaiso buildings were not the only physical space that was leased for local education; notably a similar arrangement was established in Portage, Indiana in 2012 – but that ultimately suffered the same fate as the larger Valparaiso initiative.[68] The push for securing students in Porter County was also no doubt halted with plans of merging the Purdue North Central and Purdue University Calumet campuses.

The first new campus building under Chancellor Dworkin, the North Central Veterinary Emergency Center was the last expansion originated under the Alspaugh era. The vet center was a combined initiative of private investors, made up of 36 private local veterinarians who completely funded the endeavor. Creating an after-hours veterinarian center was of interest to the veterinarian community due to the lack of such a facility in the region. Until the building opened, locals had to travel either to Chicago or West Lafayette for emergency care.[69] The only contribution that PNC made was in the form of the physical land which belonged to the university.[70] The grounding breaking was held on December 7, 2001, with three canines, Rudy, Reese, and Dakota, helping the officials turn over the first patches of dirt for the new facility.[71] Construction lasted until March 15, 2003, with the 10,000 square foot building costing $1.4 million for the team of private individuals.[72] The vet center was the first new building opened under Dworkin, and the first new building for PNC since the Technology Building.

Overall, the usefulness of the North Center Veterinary Center was

The North Central Veterinary Emergency Center opened in 2003 as a joint venture between PNC, the Purdue School of Veterinary Medicine and a group of 36 area veterinarians. (PNW Archives)

felt more by the community at-large than for the students and staff at PNC.[73] The center was a nice addition for the overall community though, offering the only major facility for animal surgery between Chicago and West Lafayette, and becoming even more useful on March 28, 2011, when the center was officially opened for continuous operation.[74] Given that PNC only contributed some land to the operation, the advantages outweigh the only negative, having less land for future expansion of the university, a commodity the university had in abundance.

Another important addition to PNC was the creation of the University Park Apartments by private investors across the street from the campus. Announced in September of 2003, the apartments were a completely privately funded endeavor from South Coast LLC., headed by Harley Snyder and James Combs who received 37 acres of land from the Purdue Research Foundation, with an additional nine acres given to the project by the Kesling and Rocke Orthodontic Group.[75] The goal of the apartments was to create a more traditional college atmosphere for students by providing an amenity that many other college campuses had — housing. "We're like 10 miles away from everywhere," Dworkin commented before he dug a shiny silver spade into the dirt. "We want to make this more of a campus for our full-time students."[76] The private

University Village included 160 apartments and a clubhouse, as well as 44 single-family homes and 12 duplexes accommodating 24 living units. (PNW Archives)

housing endeavor served as an examination of demand for housing on campus: with enough demand the idea of actual, Purdue funded dormitories would be created. The 2008 Strategic Master Plan even included residential housing on campus as a part of its expansion prospects for the university.[77] The apartments became functional fairly quickly, providing the first phase of housing opportunities to students and the general public by the fall of 2005.[78]

The University Park Apartments had some drawbacks following completion. Since the apartments were not technically affiliated with PNC, although clearly aimed at university students by the name, the rate of students actually utilizing the space has changed throughout the years, especially when faced with the merger of the two regional Purdue campuses in Northwest Indiana. Brittany Piaseczny, the Assistant Business Manager for the apartment complex stated that in 2009 around four of the ten apartment buildings were used for student housing, but since the merger in 2016, that rate has dropped significantly, "Since 2016 when the merging began for the Purdue North Central and Purdue Calumet [*sic*] we began to lose a lot of our students and athletes." As of the fall semester of 2018, she stated that only one building of the ten is dedicated to Purdue students, around 50 total beds.[79] In hindsight the bigger gain in terms of housing opportunities was for the local community, as only ten percent of the buildings are utilized by Purdue affiliates. Further, since the inception of the apartments, there have been numerous instances of underage drinking, driving while under the influence, and other alcohol related events at the apartments or the surrounding area by PNC students. One newspaper summarized the situation in 2006 saying, "Since the housing units went up, it's been a magnet for underage drinking parties."[80] Some 59 students had been arrested or issued citations for underage drinking since the apartments opened and

Gathering before the statue of a running arch for a "photo-op" became a tradition with PNC graduates. (PNW Archives)

two individuals were charged with driving while under the influence.[81] Other incidents included a drunken fight over a slice of pizza by two PNC baseball players in 2006 and a drunk PNC student having his leg impaled after a second story balcony collapsed during his twenty-first birthday party.[82] It is important to note that the apartments are private property, thus out of the purview of PNC. The University Park Apartments gave the commuter campus of PNC student housing, but also contributed to alcohol related incidents and has been much more of an asset to the wider community due to low student rates of use.

Finally, Chancellor Dworkin helped to create the fourth major building at PNC, a Student Services and Activities Complex that was named for him shortly before it was officially opened on May 24, 2016. The story of the eventual Dworkin Center began long before he came to Westville in 2000. It was one of Chancellor Alspaugh's biggest regrets: "I wish we'd been able to get a gym and a theater," Alspaugh said. "Several years ago, we had a proposal for this, but it didn't get funded."[83] The idea could even be traced back farther, former professor and State Senator Anita Bowser spent decades lobbying for PNC to build a large group assembly building saying just days before her death, "I have been working on getting this project since 1950, when I produced

"Pounce the Panther" served as the mascot for PNC athletic teams. (PNW Archives)

a George Kaufman play for the school." Bowser's plea helped pass the initial funding of $1 million for planning of the center in 2007. Between the initial funding and the final state release of funds, the building took different shapes and locations.[84] It was not until May of 2013 that state funding for the project was finally released to Purdue, and the ground-breaking did not take place until October 16, 2014. Costing $33.4 million to complete, with about 70 percent of the funding coming from the state, while the remaining came from private donations and fundraisers, including $1 million donations from Dr. Peter Kesling and a donor who wished to stay anonymous; with the remaining amount coming from "student activity fees."[85] The finished building consisted of 86,000 square feet of space, including study/group meeting rooms, a recreation center, workout areas, an indoor track, a double basketball court, and a conference hall for events.[86] The center was to provide a home for PNC sports teams, a recreation center/lounge area for students, and a large scale meeting place for community events and commencements.

The need for the facility was evident for years. In 2006 a report titled "Space Utilization Committee Report and Recommendations" stated that "A multi-purpose building is urgently needed for student activities and athletics and community engagement efforts." But the timing of the building has brought about questions regarding its usefulness, especially in light of the merger between PNC and Purdue Calumet. The building was intended to house PNC athletics, a much needed priority. However, the merger completely changed the athletics picture. All six PNC sports teams merged with Purdue Calumet's teams in the fall of 2016, effectively halving the number of team positions, coaches, and administrators. The location of the unified teams changed as well. Most now practice mainly at Purdue Calumet. As the Associate Athletic Director for Compliance, Tom Albano, explained, this is due to the availa-

This aerial view of the mature campus as it appeared shortly after construction of the Veterinary Emergency Center shows the three main campus buildings to the left with the veterinary center to the left of the baseball field in the upper right. (PNW Archives)

bility of student housing through Purdue dormitories and not the private student housing option in Westville. Of the thirteen unified sports teams, only five play any home games in Westville. This consisted of half of the home games for men's basketball, women's basketball, women's volleyball, and one meet per year for men's and women's cross country. It should be noted that for the 2018 sports seasons, women's volleyball played three home games in Westville and five at Hammond, while men's and women's basketball played six home games in Westville compared to seven in Hammond.[87] Moreover, the official decision during the merger to unify the sports teams and finalize details like practice and home game locations was not finalized until after ground was broken on the new complex on October 16, 2014. However, evidence from the September 2, 2014, "Faculty Workshop on Unification Issues" in Westville indicated that the participants were still broadly discussing athletics: "What will happen with athletics after the unification? What team sports will be available for students, both intercollegiate and intermural?"[88] Even the Unification Committee Minutes of July 10, 2015 still indicated lingering questions about student athletics:

PNW will have a combined total of 13 intercollegiate teams. Many issues will need to be resolved including playing time, grade expectations, etc. A concern was raised about students and driving time between home and the practice facility being used in addition to any legal issues surrounding this.[89]

Chancellor Dworkin denied any such hesitation or lack of planning or execution before the merger announcement. Still, other sources clearly paint a different picture of the preparedness of PNW's sports merger, which bring up lingering questions regarding the Dworkin Center. Spending $33.4 million without full knowledge of the details of PNW athletics appears rash. Without a clear view of what would happen as a result of unification the ground breaking should have been delayed.[90]

Furthermore, another major reason for the creation of the Dworkin Center was the opportunity for students to graduate on their home campus. The delays in releasing funds allowed only one class to graduate as PNC before the merger took effect, and even this had to be held before the building was officially opened.[91] Afterwards it could be argued that students attending the Westville campus of PNW would have had the opportunity to graduate from their own campus without the new building, as the Hammond campus had existing facilities to accommodate Purdue Calumet students, and after the merger, both campuses. Although Westville-based students would have had to drive to Hammond for commencement, the potential cost savings might have outweighed the once-in-their-collegiate-career drive to Hammond, especially since one of the primary focuses of the merger was cost-savings by reducing redundancies like having two chancellors and two of the same sports teams. Having two gymnasiums appears to be an obvious redundancy, as does the creation of a larger workout facility when PNC already had such facilities, albeit smaller, in the ground floor remodel of the LSF Building, and when hindsight has shown that PNC athletes primarily practice at Hammond.

The worth of the center for community involvement has been useful to the campus. Since its creation, events like the Sinai Forum have been relocated from area buildings to the Dworkin Center. It is important to note that the headlining speaker for the 2018 season, former FBI Director James Comey, and 2019 speaker General John F. Kelly, had to still be held externally from PNW Westville; taking place at the Blue Chip Casino in Michigan City. Such an act makes one question if large community events might have already outgrown the new building.[92]

The Dworkin Center was not the only building to be planned for Westville. The same 2006 "Space Utilization Committee Report and Recommendations" highlighted the need for a fourth classroom building for modern science labs, increased classroom space, and additional offices.[93] The potential building was in serious talks, with the Purdue

Board of Trustees approving $33.4 million for its construction in 2012 – notably the same amount that the Dworkin Center eventually cost. With the merger potentially satisfying some of the original need for the Dworkin Center, perhaps priorities should have shifted, although state money was already discharged for the Center and private donations had already been given. The sharp decline in Westville enrollment since February of 2014 — a 42 percent drop in core enrollment from the fall 2014 semester (3,287) to the fall 2018 semester (1,906) — has since made the need for expansion of classroom space moot.[94]

The timing of the merger into PNW complicated Dworkin Center construction, however it is important to note that the ground breaking for the center (October 16, 2014) was a full seven months *after* the public announcement of the merger. During this time serious reevaluation of its usefulness, or the realization of the uncertainty of the athletic teams, should have led to a delay of, reimagining, or even cancellation of the project. This was never done.

Chancellor Dworkin's time at PNC left profound changes to the regional campus. He oversaw large community involvement initiatives that gained local support for the institution, transitioned PNC away from associate degrees and into bachelor degrees, shifted student demographics, and added to the infrastructure of the campus. Yet, it is important to note that these shifts were not in isolation. For example, the achievement of academic autonomy led to the increase in baccalaureate degrees which, in turn, helped increase enrollment and graduation rates and even helped to justify the building additions and remodels. Such intersectionality was key to the transformation of PNC. Ultimately Chancellor Dworkin led Purdue North Central to success and eventually — through the merger — its end.

---

[1] "Purdue University North Central Commencement," May 16, 2016, Archive and Special Collection, Box 1, PNW Archives.

[2] John Nicholas, "PNC Chancellor to Stay-for a While," *Tribune* (South Bend, IN), June, 29, 1999, Press Clippings Collection, Box: 2006 Press Clippings, PNWArchives.

[3] "James Dworkin" Purdue University: Krannert School of Management. Accessed November 29, 2018, https://krannert.purdue.edu/directory/bio.php?username=jdworkin; Stan Maddux, "More's the Word for New Purdue North Central Boss," *Post-Tribune* (Chicago, IL), Jan. 14, 2000.

[4] James Dworkin, interview by Joshua W. Koepke, Nov. 12, 2018, West Lafayette, IN (hereafter Dworkin interview).

[5] Dworkin, interview.

[6] Purdue University, *Perspective* (Fall 2008, 13; Sasaki Associates Inc., "Purdue University North Central Master Plan Report," November 2008, Strategic Plan Collection, Box 1, File 51, PNW Archives.

[7] "Mayor Names Jeff Jones to Board," *News-Dispatch* (Michigan City, IN), Oct. 19, 2002.

[8] Richard Chambers, "Burgwald Seeking Re-Election to School Board," *News-Dispatch*, Aug. 17, 2014.

[9] "Michigan City Area Chamber of Commerce Announces 2014 Board Members and Officers," *NWI Times* (Munster, IN), Jan. 27, 2014.

[10] Dworkin interview.

[11] "United Way is Set to Recognize PNC," *Times* (Munster, IN), Feb. 23, 2009.

[12] Dworkin, interview; Amanda Bishop, "Terrific Deal for Selected MC Students," *Herald-Argus*, Jan. 28, 2004; Deborah Sederberg, "Organizations Donate to College Bound Fund," *News-Dispatch*, June 5, 2004; Amanda Haverstick, "City Savings Bank of Michigan City has Joined the College Bound Program with a Five-Year Financial Commitment for $25,000," *News-Dispatch*, Feb. 18, 2005; "PNC College Bound Partnership," *Beacher* (Michigan City, IN), 46, March 30, 2006; "Wells Fargo Donation to Aid Qualifying Students," *News Dispatch*, Oct. 26, 2006; "PNC Chancellor Awarded," *Beacher*, Oct. 23, 2014.

[13] Daniel Przybyla, "Joined Together: A Better Future Targeted by New Alliance," *Herald Argus*, Feb. 21, 2004; Dworkin, interview.

[14] Stan Maddux, "Bus Service Stays Optimistic," *NWI Times*, Feb. 19, 2015.

[15] "Transit Triangle Offers Convenient Travel," *Indicator,* July 9, 2015, 3; Stan Maddux, "Bus Service to PNC Approved," *NWI Times*, Oct. 17, 2014.

[16] Dworkin, interview.

[17] Catherine LaFrance, "PNC Partners with Sinai," *Herald-Argus*, August, 8, 2006; "Woodward Kicks off Forum Season," *News-Dispatch*, August 28, 2006; Doug Ross, "Comey Defends Decision in 2016 Clinton Announcement at Sinai Forum in Michigan City," *NWI Times*, Sept. 9, 2018.

[18] George T. Asteriadis and Debra A. Nielsen, eds., "Faculty Handbook for Academic Promotion and Tenure" (Westville, IN: PNC, 2005), 4-8.

[19] "Higher Learning Commission Self-Study" (Westville, IN: PNC, 2011), 100.

[20] "Petition for Campus Academic Autonomy," August 16, 2005, 6, Scrapbooks Collection, Box: "PNC Autonomy History '62-'06," PNW Archives.

[21] Dworkin, interview.

[22] Cynthia Roberts, interview by Joshua W. Koepke, Nov. 2, 2018, Valparaiso, IN.

[23] Stan Maddux, "More's the Word for New Purdue North Central Boss," *Post Tribune,* (Chicago, Il.), Jan. 14, 2000.

[24] "Purdue Campus to Offer Bachelor's in Nursing," *Tribune,* (South Bend, IN), Feb. 22, 2004; "Business Classes Offered," *News-Dispatch*, August 5, 2001; "PNC to Offer New Engineering Degree," *News-Dispatch*, Nov. 13, 2007; "PNC to Offer 2 New Degree Programs," *News-Dispatch*, May 15, 2012;

"PNC Offering Bachelor's in Human Resources," *NWI Times*, Feb. 23, 2009; "Childhood Education Program Recognized," *NWI Times*, March 27, 2014; Deborah Sederberg, "PNC to Offer New Degrees," *News-Dispatch*, May 19, 2001; "PNC Adds Social Work Degree," *Leader* (Knox, IN), Oct. 29, 2009.

[25] James Dworkin, "Guest Commentary: PNC Career Always About Student Access, Success," *NWI Times* (Munster, IN), June 26, 2016.

[26] Virginia R. Allen, Barbara Ann Bardes, et al, "Report of a Visit to Purdue University North Central for the Higher Learning Commission of the North Central Association of Colleges and Schools," April 25, 2001, 6. Booklets Collection, PNW Archives.

[27] Robert L. Ringel, email message to James Dworkin, Dec. 18, 2000, Scrapbooks Collection, Box: "PNC Autonomy History '62-'06," PNW Archives; Rick A. Richards, "PNC Receives 'Full Academic Autonomy,'" *News-Dispatch*, Feb. 8, 2006.

[28] Ibid.

[29] "PNC Curriculum Revisions Help Students Earn Degrees," *Herald-Argus*, May 17, 2012.

[30] "PNC Approved to Change 'Divisions' to 'Colleges,'" *NWI Times*, June 10, 2006.

[31] Erik Lords, "With a New Community-College System, Indiana Hopes for More Skilled Workers," *Chronicle of Higher Education*, August 18, 2000.

[32] Olivia Clarke, "Governor Expands Community College System," *NWI Times*, Oct. 6, 2004.

[33] Brain Williams, "Ivy Tech Shows Off New Digs," *NWI Times*, May 26, 2006.

[34] Stan Maddux, "More's the Word for New Purdue North Central Boss," *Post Tribune* (Chicago, Il.), Jan. 14, 2000.

[35] "Purdue University North Central: Focused Visit Report 2003," 2003, 64, Booklets Collection, PNW Archives.

[36] "Alspaugh Proud of Improvements in Quality, Service: Retired Administrator saw North Central through Rapid Growth," *Inside Purdue*, January 25, 2000, 8.

[37] "Purdue University North Central Commencement," May 9, 2000, Commencement Collection, Box: Commencements 1990-2009, PNW Archives; Dan Petreikis, "Purdue University North Central Holds Forty-Eight Commencement Ceremony In New Campus Expansion," *Valpolife.com*, May 17, 2016.

[38] Elizabeth Holmes, "Ivy Tech, PNC Sign Partnership Agreement," *NWI Times*, March 30, 2006.

[39] Jeff Jones, "Purdue North Central Enrollment Continues to Set Records," September 1, 2000, News Releases PNC Collection, Box: 5, File: 358 Sep. 2000, PNW Archives; Amanda Bishop, "PNC's Enrollment Rises Slightly Over Last Year," *Herald-Argus*, Sept. 10, 2001; Carol Connelly, "Purdue North Central Sets Enrollment Record," Aug. 28, 2002, News Releases PNC Collection, Box: 5, File: 383 Aug. 2002, PNW Archives; Carol Connelly, "PNC Increases Full-Time Student Numbers," Sept. 9, 2003, News Releases PNC Collection, Box: 5, File: 397 Sep. 2003, PNW Archives; Carole Carlson,

"Valparaiso University Records Largest Hike Among Area Colleges," *Post Tribune*, Sept. 29, 2004; "PNC Increases Student Numbers, Sets Credit Hours Record," *The Voice*, Aug. 20, 2005; "PNC Sets Record for Enrollment," *Herald-Argus*, Sept. 6, 2006; "PNC Enrollment at All-Time High," *News Dispatch*, Sept. 4, 2007; "PNC Sets Enrollment and Credit Hour Records," *Indicator*, Sept. 18, 2008; "PNC Sets Enrollment Record," *Beacher*, 36, Sept. 17, 2009; "PNC Sets Enrollment Records," *News Dispatch*, Sept. 2, 2010; "PNC Sets Enrollment, Credit Hour Records," *Herald-Argus*, Sept. 13, 2011; "PNC Sets Enrollment Record," *Herald-Argus*, Aug. 30, 2012; "PNC Sets Enrollment and Credit Hour Records," *Indicator*, Sept. 19, 2013; "Purdue North Central Sets Enrollment Record," *Herald-Argus*, Sept.12, 2014; "PNC has Slight Decrease in Enrollment Numbers," *News Dispatch*, Sept. 25, 2015; "Enrollment Summary Report: Fall 2016," Purdue University Northwest, Sept. 15, 2017, 1-5; "Enrollment Summary Report – Fall 2017," Purdue University Northwest, Sept. 14, 2017, 1-6. https://www.pnw.edu/planning-institutional-effectiveness/wp-content/uploads/sites/48/ENROLLMENT_SUMMARY_REPORT_ FALL _2017_0914.pdf.; "Enrollment Summary Report – Fall 2018," Purdue University Northwest, Sept. 19, 2018, 1-7, https://www.pnw.edu/planning-institutional-effectiveness/wp-content/uploads/sites/48/ENROLLMENT_SUM MARY_REPORT_ FALL_2018_0903.pdf; Fall semester data was used to create the graph due to the general use of fall semester on enrollment data graphs, virtually all spring semesters receive small drops to enrollment numbers compared to their corresponding fall semester.

[40] "Purdue University Northwest Interactive Fact Book," Purdue University Northwest, 2018. https://www.pnw.edu/planning-institutional-effectiveness/factbook/.

[41] "PNC Sets Enrollment Records," *News Dispatch*, Sept. 2, 2010; "PNC has Slight Decrease in Enrollment Numbers," *News Dispatch*, Sept. 25, 2015.

[42] "Historic Enrollment by Degree Type," PowerPoint prepared by the PNW office of the Vice Chancellor for Administration, 2019.

[43] "Higher Learning Commission Self-Study" (2011), 22, PNW Archives.

[44] Sue Loughlin, "IDOC Changing Inmate Education: Along with Funding Degrees to Focus on Employment," *Tribune-Star,* Press Clippings Collection, File: May 2011, PNW Archives.

[45] "Record Enrollment Puts PNC Campus at Top Tier," *Post Tribune*, Sept. 21, 2006; Robert Rich, "The Great Recession," *Federal Reserve History*, Nov. 22, 2013.

[46] "IUN Sees Enrollment Increase," *Post-Tribune*, Sept. 12, 2009.

[47] "PNC has Slight Decrease in Enrollment Numbers," *News Dispatch*, September 25, 2015; Jeff Jones, "Purdue North Central Enrollment Continues to Set Records," September 1, 2000, News Releases PNC Collection, Box: 5, File: 358 Sept. 2000, PNW Archives.

[48] "Higher Learning Commission Self-Study" (Westville, IN: PNC, 2011), 56.

[49] "PNC Offers Tuition Discount Program," *Herald-Argus*, March 13, 2014.

[50] "PNC Tuition Discount Program Tallies $100,000 in Student Savings," *Indicator*, August 7, 2014, Press Clippings Collection, File: August 2014, PMW Archives.

[51] "Integrated Postsecondary Education Data System (IPEDS) Report," National Center for Education Statistics, for 2010, 2012, 2014.

[52] Brian Williams, "Purdue Board Oks $1.1B for its Schools: Trustees Meet at PNC to Discuss Budget Woes," *NWI Times*, April 10, 2010.

[53] Carmen McCollum, "Schools Focused on College Completion: Commission Report Details Grad Rates," *NWI Times*, Feb. 19, 2014, A5.

[54] Mat Fritz, "Daniels Addresses Issues at PNC," *News Dispatch*, April 27, 2012.

[55] Dworkin interview; "PNC Offers Tuition Discount Programs," *NWI Times*, June 29, 2015, A7.

[56] Dworkin interview.

[57] "Eleven Public Universities with the Worst Graduation Rates," *The Fiscal Times*, May 17, 2012.

[58] Stan Maddux, "More's the Word for New Purdue North Central Boss," *Post Tribune*, Jan. 14, 2000; Azure Domschke, "New PNC Chancellor Wants New Buildings," *NWI Times*, Jan. 14, 2000.

[59] "PNC Establishes Indiana Dunes Research Station," *News Dispatch*, July 13, 2000; Michael McArdle, "Purdue Field Station Finds Home Inside Dunes," *Post Tribune*, July 12, 2000.

[60] Azure Domschke, "Technology Building Renovations Complete: New Labs, Classrooms, Offices will be Open for Full Semester," *NWI Times*, June 5, 2000.

[61] "Institutional Self-Study" (2001), 131, PNW Archives.

[62] Charles M. Bartholomew, "New Activity Center Awaits PNC Students," *Post Tribune*, July 11, 2001; Deborah Werner, "PNC Opens New Student Facility in Library," *NWI Times*, Press Clippings Collection, File: July 2001, PNW Archives; Deborah Sederberg, "PNC Project Benefits Students," *News Dispatch*, July 11, 2001; "Higher Learning Commission Self-Study" (2011), 12, PNW Archives.

[63] Azure Domschke, "Valparaiso Academic Center will Offer Undergraduate Courses, Business Training," *Times*, Sept. 12, 2000.

[64] "Valpo's PUNC Site Gets a Name Change," *Post Tribune*, Feb. 25, 2006.

[65] "Higher Learning Commission Self-Study" (2011), 5, PNW Archives.

[66] James D. Wolf Jr., "Purdue Campus in Valpo Gets Old Ivy Tech Parking," *Post Tribune*, Jan. 23, 2009.

[67] Letter, L. James Salle to Deborah Kohler, April 28, 2016. Emailed copy of letter given to author.

[68] Joyce Russell, "Portage Inks PNC Lease: University Will Use Two Classrooms in University Center," *NWI Times*, Nov. 30, 2012.

[69] Amanda Bishop, "Groundbreaking for PNC Veterinary Center," *Herald-Argus*, June, 2002.

[70] Dworkin, interview.

[71] James B. Dworkin, "Exciting Change Coming to PNC," *News Dispatch*, Nov. 15, 2001; Carole Carlson, "PUNC, Dogs Break Ground," *Post Tribune*, Dec. 8, 2001.

[72] Courtney Castle and Julia Johnson, "For After-Hours Veterinary Care, Go to Emergency Clinic," *NWI Times*, June 8, 2003; Amanda Bishop, "When Your Dog Turns Blue and it's After Hours," *Herald-Argus*, March 6, 2003.

[73] Amanda Bishop, "Groundbreaking for PNC Veterinary Center," *Herald -Argus*, June, 2002, Press Clippings Collection, June 2002, PNW Archives.

[74] "North Central Veterinary Center to Open 24/7 on March 28," *Indicator*, March 24, 2011.

[75] Carole Carlson, "Enrollment Up: Number of Students Increasing despite Higher Tuition," *Post Tribune*, Sept. 30, 2003; "Purdue North Central Plans $30 Million Housing Project," *Chesterton Tribune*, Sept. 23, 2003; Carole Carlson, "PNC Discloses Housing Plans: Proposed Development Would Have 150 Apartments," *Post Tribune*, Sept. 23, 2003.

[76] Carole Carlson, "Students as Residents: Purdue University North Central Building Student-Apartment Complex," *Post Tribune*, Oct. 6, 2004.

[77] Sasaki Associates Inc., "Purdue University North Central Master Plan Report," November 2008, Strategic Plan Collection, Box 1, File 51: November 2008, PNW Archives.

[78] Deborah Sederberg, "Apartments Across from PNC Filling Up," *News Dispatch*, Sept. 12, 2005.

[79] Brittany Piaseczny, email message to author, Oct. 3, 2018.

[80] Stan Maddux, "Cops Raid Two Parties near PNC, Arrest 17," *Post-Tribune*, Sept. 23, 2006, Scrapbook Collection, Box: Scrapbook, File: PNC Off -Campus Market Housing; University Village, PNW Archives.

[81] "Seven Arrested Playing 'Beer Pong,'" *Herald-Argus*, August 25, 2006; "19 Arrested at Parties near PNC," *Herald-Argus*, Sept. 22, 2006; Stan Maddux, "Underage Party-Goers End Night with Arrests," *Post Tribune*, Nov. 28, 2006; Jason Miller, "Party Leads to Arrests," *News Dispatch*, Nov. 10, 2007; "PNC Students Arrested at Party," *News Dispatch*, Jan. 21, 2009; Stan Maddux, "Authorities: Underage Drinking Party Busted: Eight Cited for Alcohol, and Officers Pour Drinks Down the Kitchen Sink," *Times*, April 6, 2011; "Minors Cited at PNC Apartments," *Herald-Argus*, Nov. 17, 2006.

[82] "PNC Baseball Players Fight Over Pizza," *Herald-Argus*, May 8, 2006; Stan Maddux, "Westville Area Man Falls From Second-Floor Balcony during Party," *Times*, Sept. 16, 2013.

[83] "Alspaugh Proud of Improvements in Quality, Service: Retired Administrator saw North Central through Rapid Growth," *Inside Purdue*, January 25, 2000, 8.

[84] Deborah Sederberg, "PNC Building was a Priority for Bowser," *News Dispatch*, March 6, 2007.

[85] "PNC to Celebrate Groundbreaking on October 16," *Indicator*, October 2, 2014, 3; James D. Wolf Jr., "PNC Breaks Ground on new Student Complex," *Post Tribune*, October 17, 2014; Stan Maddux, "Funds Freed for PNC Activities Site: Facility Offering Home for Athletic Teams and Recreation," *Times*, May 2, 2013.

PURDUE UNIVERSITY NORTH CENTRAL

[86] Jessica O'Brien, "New PNW Complex Opens," *Herald-Argus*, May 25, 2016.

[87] "PNW Athletics," Accessed January 14, 2019. http://www.pnwathletics. com/.

[88] Purdue University North Central Faculty Senate, "Faculty Senate Document 14-01," Sept. 2, 2014, 2-3, https://faculty.pnw.edu/senate-north-central/ wp-content/uploads/sites/3/2014/09/14-01-Report-from-the-Faculty-Workshop -on-Issues-Surrounding-Unification.pdf.

[89] Debbie Nielsen, "Unification Committee Meeting," July 10, 2015, Uploaded August 26, 2015 by Petersor, https://www.pnw.edu/unification-archive/2015/08/26/unification-committee-meeting-071015/.

[90] Dworkin interview, "Purdue University Calumet University Senate Meeting Minutes," March 5, 2014, 4, http://faculty.pnw.edu/senate-calumet/wp -content/uploads/sites/2/2014/03/FacultySenateMinutesMarch14.doc.

[91] "Purdue University North Central Commencement," May 16, 2016, PNW Archive and Special Collection, Box 1, PNW Archives.

[92] James Comey opens Purdue University Northwest Sinai Forum's 65th Season," April 16, 2018, https://pnw.edu/news/james-comey-opens-purdue-university-northwest-sinai-forums-65th-season/; "Geopolitics: Risk, Reward and Balance," https://www.pnw.edu/sinai-forum/geopolitics-risk-reward-and-balance/

[93] "Space Utilization Committee Report and Recommendations," May 1, 2006, Booklets Collection, PNW Archives.

[94] See figure 2.

UNIFICATION:

"AN OVERARCHING THEME OF BROKEN PROMISES"

James S. Pula

The beginning of the end for Purdue North Central came on February 26, 2014, with the formal announcement that the Purdue University Board of Trustees had approved the merger of PNC with Purdue Calumet in Hammond.[1] The stated purpose of what became known as "unification" was the reduction of administrative costs by replacing two sets of chancellors, deans, and other upper administration with a single organizational structure that would eliminate costly duplication. Officially, the request for consolidation submitted to the regional accrediting association stated: "The purpose of the unification is to combine resources and eliminate duplication where possible. Through the larger scale of the combined institutions, the two institutions also hope to provide enhanced programmatic options for students and more opportunities for community engagement and increased collaboration for research and other purposes."[2] At the same time, there was a promise that the savings would be used to provide additional support for students and faculty.[3]

THE PROCESS OF UNIFICATION

When President Mitch Daniels and the Trustees announced the planned unification into the new Purdue University Northwest, administrators and faculty received about one year to make the transition. Committees formed to address issues such as the administrative organization of the new university, developing a consolidated Faculty Senate constitution and bylaws, creating a single promotion and tenure document, and making all of the necessary alterations in curricula, course descriptions, and other requirements to merge the academic programs. For these tasks the two campuses each formed committees that met jointly with their counterparts on the other campus to draft proposals each could support.[4] The two existing Faculty Senates then considered the resulting recommendations, each acting separately, for approval so that each campus agreed to the proposals before the formal unification date in the hope of smoothing the unification as much as possible. Given the differing campus characteristics and temperaments, coupled with the fact that very few faculty from either campus knew their new colleagues from the other, it was a tribute to faculty dedication that considerable progress was made with minimal friction.

For a two-year transition period there was to be equal representation of the two campuses in the Faculty Senate, largely to assuage concerns in Westville that PNC faculty would have little voice given the fact that Hammond faculty (Purdue Calumet) outnumbered them by more than three to one. Senate committees were populated by faculty from both campuses. To address concerns about promotion and tenure, review committees were purposely skewed so that any candidate would be reviewed by a majority of people from the person's home campus; for example, if the Primary Committee contained five members, three would be from the candidate's home campus. This was believed to protect all faculty during the initial years when colleagues on the two campuses were only just meeting and beginning to interact with each other. Both of these approaches — the Faculty Senate and promotion and tenure policies and procedures — worked well for the first two years, following which the transition policies gave way to normal proportional election by the various departments regardless of the faculty member's "home campus."

Although the unification committees accomplished their tasks within the original one-year timeframe, the overall timetable for unification was inadequate. Since the new PNW Faculty Senate could not legally convene until after the formal approval of unification by its accrediting agency,[5] the myriad of policies and procedures required to conduct normal business, particularly as it related to curricular and other academic policies, took up much of its time during its first year of existence to the detriment of other important matters. In fact, as the second year of unification concluded, the Senate was still addressing issues where the new PNW did not have approved unified policies to cover academic/student issues. For example, there was no unified policy on experiential learning, nor any single policy on how to handle credits earned for military service. These and other such academic policy issues, along with the need to create a new promotion and tenure document for use after the initial transitional period, occupied nearly all of the Faculty Senate's time during the second and third years of unification.

IMPLEMENTATION ISSUES

There are times when even the best of planning encounters difficulties. In an attempt to solve the distance issue — the campuses were 42 miles apart — PNW rented a meeting facility in Portage close to the midpoint between the two campuses. Meetings of the Faculty Senate, department meetings, committees, and other such events could utilize the facility to minimize the need for travel. Further, the university began a free shuttle bus service for people to travel between the campuses, including the Portage facility. This was beneficial in minimizing travel to meetings, but the facility was too small for use by classes and the bus service, while helpful, required a roundtrip of about two and one half to three hours to move students and faculty between campuses. This made it in large part ineffective for students who wished to enroll in a course on the opposite campus.

One of the obvious factors to consider in merging two distant campuses is the respective campus cultures. Hammond and Westville are two very different campuses. The former was at the time of unification an urban campus claiming, in 2012, 9,405 students with dormitories and a sizable number of commuter students, most of the latter living close by in the surrounding community. Because of its size and the urban, residential nature of the campus, student life was much more developed, as was the supporting infrastructure for student activities and events. Westville was quite different. With no dormitories, located in a rural area with no regular bus or other connections to the surrounding towns, it was exclusively a commuter campus. Its 2012 enrollment of 3,573 core degree-seeking students were seldom on campus except when they attended classes. Further, its size meant that in some of its degree programs the junior-senior level courses were relatively small, although overall enrollment in its degree programs was sufficient to keep the budget "in the black."[6]

With the merging of two campuses, each of which had its own separate, established identity, into a single new entity, it was important to promote a single, unified image for the new Purdue University Northwest. Because of this, advertising and public statements emphasized the "one university" idea. Promoting the new university as a single organization was not inherently problematic but it ignored the growing concern among residents in the Westville service area — Porter, LaPorte, and Starke Counties — for the future of their campus. Rumors circulated that Westville was to become a two-year institution, or even that it was to be closed with the campus sold to Ivy Tech Community College. Since all of the administrative offices of Purdue Northwest were located in Hammond, effectively leaving no one in charge on the Westville campus, and advertising emphasized "one university," there was no effective antidote to the negative perception. The resulting unease in the communities served by the Westville campus led some potential students to reconsider enrolling at an institution they believed might not exist much longer.[7]

Equally detrimental was the uniform application by Provost Ralph

Mueller of the "one university" maxim to academic affairs. Without considering the differences in the two campuses, the PNW academic administrators imposed a minimum size limit on courses with the result that a higher percentage of upper level classes began to be canceled on the Westville campus. This not only caused concern among students about completing their degrees, but further reinforced apprehensions in the local community about the future of the Westville campus. Similarly, the elimination of the Westville MBA program through its incorporation into a Hammond program had the same effect. The Westville program was a hybrid of online work with Saturday classes designed to meet the needs of working adults. The Hammond program was much more traditional. As might be expected, the change in program and location led to a decline in enrollment from 39 students in fall 2015 to only 8 in fall 2018.[8] Changes in other Westville programs occasioned by adopting the Hammond models, coupled with the dictum on course minimums, quickly made it difficult for Westville students in some programs to complete their degree requirements. In turn, this negative publicity discouraged some potential students from enrolling since they would have to travel a considerable distance to complete their degrees in Hammond.

Following the initial announcement of unification, students on both campuses were understandably anxious about what the changes would mean for them. Those in Westville were especially nervous about whether they would be able to complete their degree programs. To address the many questions emerging from students and the surrounding communities, PNW issued a brochure titled "Student and Parent FAQs Purdue University Northwest," the contents of which it also placed on its website in October 2015. One portion of both of these documents read as follows:

Q: I am enrolled at the Purdue North Central campus. Will I have to attend classes at the Calumet campus?

A: As a student at the Purdue North Central campus, you will attend classes at North Central. However, you may have the opportunity in coming semesters to choose to take some classes offered at Calumet. Some online courses already are shared across the two campuses.[9]

Despite the promise that students would not have to travel to complete their degree, within a year of unification the PNW administration disavowed this pledge and advisors in some majors were openly telling students they would have to commute to Hammond. For Westville stu-

Student and Parent

FAQs

Purdue University Northwest

PURDUE
UNIVERSITY
CALUMET

PURDUE
UNIVERSITY
NORTH CENTRAL

Pending the approval of the Higher Learning Commission, Purdue University Northwest (PNW) will be established through the unification of Purdue University Calumet and Purdue University North Central. Students admitted for semesters beginning Fall 2016 will be students of Purdue University Northwest, a regional university within the Purdue University system with two campuses in Hammond and Westville, Indiana.

Q: *I am enrolled at the Purdue North Central campus, will I need to travel to Purdue Calumet to receive service and assistance?*

A: No, both campuses will provide full service to students. Examples include admissions, financial aid, registration, payment, career services, academic advising, library services, tutoring, testing, disability services, student activities and other support activities.

Q: *I am enrolled at the Purdue Calumet campus, will I have to attend classes at the North Central campus?*

A: No. As a student at the Purdue Calumet campus, you will attend classes at Calumet. However, you may have the opportunity in coming semesters to choose to take some classes offered at PNC. Some online courses already are shared across the two campuses.

Q: *I am enrolled at the Purdue North Central campus. Will I have to attend classes at the Calumet campus?*

A: As a student at the Purdue North Central campus, you will attend classes at North Central. However, you may have the opportunity in coming semesters to choose to take some classes offered at Calumet. Some online courses already are shared across the two campuses.

Left: The cover of the FAQ brochure issued to students to answer basic questions and reassure them about unification. Right: A panel of the brochure that specifically assured students on both the Hammond and Westville campuses that they would be able to complete their degree programs on their home campuses and not have to travel to the other campus for classes. These broken promises, along with others, created a very toxic atmosphere in the communities served by Purdue Northwest, particularly those in the Westville service area since they were the ones most often expected to travel. (PNW Archives)

dents who lived in LaPorte, Rolling Prairie, South Bend, or other areas east and south of campus, this new requirement could mean the difference between a twenty-minute commute and one of an hour and twenty minutes each way. Throw in the vagaries of winter weather and the fact that the region straddled two time zones, Eastern and Central, and the new requirement caused some students to leave and no doubt potential students to rethink their options. Perhaps even more detrimental was the obvious failure of the PNW administration to keep its earlier promises. Students rightly felt deceived, a sentiment they likely shared with their parents, siblings, and friends. When asked about the failure to honor earlier promises, the PNW administration, indifferent to growing student concerns, disingenuously responded: "Circumstances have changed."[10]

In one of the most egregious cases that harmed students, while at the same time infringing on the authority of the Faculty Senate, the administrator responsible for the teacher education program blatantly disregarded faculty authority by forcing the two people responsible for the student teaching courses to add a new requirement to their syllabi after the courses had already begun. These additions established new conditions for the successful completion of the courses without these ever being submitted for approval through the established curriculum process. The new requirements consisted of six mandatory workshops, three to be held at Hammond and three at Westville, but with all students obligated to attend all six. As a change in course content and requirements, these required approval of the Faculty Senate but were never submitted. Instead, the administrator announced that they were being imposed by "executive decision."[11]

Aside from the failure to abide by academic regulations for the changing of course and curricular requirements, these late additions to the courses placed an exceptional burden on some students whose student teaching assignments and other requirements made it very difficult to attend the workshops which were scheduled during the week, or complete the extra work they required, because of the times and distances involved. For some Westville students this would mean driving one to two hours from their student teaching assignments to attend the workshops in Hammond at 5:00 pm, then traveling back to their teaching location after the end of the workshops at 8:00 pm.[12]

Since enforcement of this new requirement could impact grades in the student teaching experience and could effect a student's graduation if the requirement was not met, some students appealed for flexibility to allow them alternate ways of completing whatever might be required such as, for example, moving the workshops to Saturdays. All sugges-

Education students protested administratively-imposed new requirements for their degree program with this online petition that obtained 75 signatures. (change.org)

tions were refused. The students appealed to the dean of the College of Humanities, Education, and Social Sciences without success, to the PNW provost without success, and to the PNW chancellor without success. The students even began an online petition signed by 75 students and took their case to the University president and Board of Trustees, also without success. Disregarding academic regulations and hurting students apparently were not seen as problems by the PNW administration. Naturally, the students effected by these changes were not happy and they certainly shared their negative experiences with their families and friends in the surrounding communities adding to the growing PNW image problems. These student frustrations were reflected in a rapid decline in enrollment in Education programs on the Westville campus where Secondary Education enrollment went from 39 in fall 2014 to 8 in fall 2018 (-79.5 percent) and Early Childhood Education went from 74 to 21 (-71.6 percent) over the same period. Although Elementary Education increased slightly by ten students, Pre Elementary Education enrollment, those planning to enter the program but not yet accepted, nearly evaporated from 107 to 1 (-99.1 percent).[13]

The result of these broken promises and disregard for students was predictable. Writing in the *Pioneer*, the PNW student newspaper, its editor, Jacob Yothment, concluded: "Since the beginning, unification has created a culture where the administration reveals news to the affected parties at the last second." Among the examples in support of this assertion the editor cited the complete disregard for the Faculty Senates in the determination of PNW's future athletic affiliation during the unification process despite the fact that the Senates held authority over student participation in intercollegiate athletics. "The decision was made to accept the invitation [to join an athletic conference] without discussing the matter with either campus's Faculty Senate. The Westville campus's Faculty Senate was so outraged at this lack of transparency that they passed a senate document asking that the invitation be suspended." In another example,

> although the new PNW Faculty Senate had authority over the academic calendar, in March 2016 classes "were cancelled so that students could attend Founder's Day at the Westville campus. This decision was made and sent to faculty members and students three days prior to Founder's Day, giving faculty members little time to rearrange their class schedules for the rest of the year. This idea was first proposed at the December Faculty Senate meeting and was strongly opposed, but the administration went through with it anyway. From the start of communication, we have seen a pattern where the university has made decisions that affect curriculum without faculty input. It has become the culture of PNW, and it is not working. ...
>
> Whether or not these decisions benefited the university as a whole in the long run, the fact remains that decisions were made that drastically affected faculty members, and faculty was not allowed a voice. Our country has a system of checks and balances which keeps the powers that be from making decisions without going through proper channels. The administration of PNW is making decisions and then listening to feedback after. It's understandable that the administration wants to get things done quickly and efficiently, ... but thus far the only thing their actions are doing is angering faculty members. Right now, many faculty members feel as though they no longer get a say in what happens in matters of curriculum. If this culture continues, faculty will continue to be kept out of the loop, and students will suffer as a result.[14]

Almost a year later, in the January 7, 2018, issue of the *Pioneer*, when asked to comment on unification Riley Owens, the Student Government chief of staff, replied: "There is an overarching theme of broken promises." He added: "People don't speak up because they are scared of repercussions."[15]

In a similar vein, faculty were told consistently that they would not be required to travel between campuses to teach courses. This pledge was broken almost immediately after unification became official. Aside from the obvious breach of faith and resulting mistrust, this imposed a serious liability on some Westville faculty. If one was hired prior to unification and purchased a home in the Westville service area there would be the same dramatic change in commuting time that students experienced. If one lived in LaPorte, for example, instead of a fifteen minute drive to campus one would be on the road for at least an hour and fifteen minutes and with traffic most likely almost an hour and one half. More in winter. The result was that to teach one course at Hammond, someone living in LaPorte would spend almost three hours on the road, twice per week, or six hours driving. At a minimum that is three-quarters of a day lost each week where faculty are not meeting with students, pursuing service activities, or conducting research. Quite naturally, this did not promote trust on the part of the faculty.

A further rift between administration and faculty occurred over the former's recurring attempts to infringe on faculty prerogatives. It is an establish principle in higher education that the faculty have authority over the curriculum and courses. The "Constitution of the Faculty of Purdue University Northwest," approved by the Board of Trustees of Purdue University, specifically gives to the Faculty the authority: "To review and approve the general requirements for the curricula of Purdue University Northwest leading toward undergraduate academic degrees" and "To develop curricula and course content."[16] Despite this, administrators almost immediately attempted to usurp these faculty prerogatives. In one case, for example, the chair of one of the departments attempted to change the fundamental nature of a course by altering its coverage parameters, modifying the course description, and unilaterally providing new learning objectives.[17] This clearly violated the provisions of the Faculty Constitution. In another case, a dean decreed that faculty in that college would be required to give a particular written assignment and that they would be required to grade it in a certain way.[18] The grading requirement further determined the nature of the assignment that must be given. As in the case of the department chair, none of this was presented to the Faculty Senate for approval; rather, it was simply announced in clear violation of the Faculty Constitution. Naturally, these unilateral actions subverting faculty authority further eroded what little confidence the faculty had in administrative leadership.

Yet another serious blow to administrative credibility, and to the community's appraisal of the new PNW, occurred in late September 2018. Although administrators had promised students they would con-

BE IT KNOWN THAT THE TRUSTEES OF

Purdue University

UPON NOMINATION OF THE FACULTY OF
PURDUE UNIVERSITY NORTH CENTRAL
HAVE GRANTED TO

SAMPLE STUDENT

THE DEGREE OF

BACHELOR OF ARTS

IN RECOGNITION OF THE FULFILLMENT OF THE
REQUIREMENTS OF THAT DEGREE
AWARDED AT WESTVILLE IN THE STATE OF INDIANA
MAY 4, 2012

CHAIRMAN OF THE TRUSTEES   PRESIDENT OF THE UNIVERSITY

Purdue University
Northwest

AND THE FACULTY OF THE
SCHOOL OF MANAGEMENT
HAVE GRANTED TO

JONATHAN SAMPLE NAME

THE DEGREE OF

BACHELOR OF SCIENCE IN ACCOUNTING
WITH HIGHEST DISTINCTION

IN RECOGNITION OF THE FULFILLMENT OF THE REQUIREMENTS OF
THAT DEGREE AWARDED BY THE PURDUE BOARD OF TRUSTEES
IN THE STATE OF INDIANA ON MAY 4, 2019.

CHAIRMAN OF THE TRUSTEES   PRESIDENT OF THE UNIVERSITY

CHANCELLOR OF
PURDUE UNIVERSITY NORTHWEST

The traditional PNC diploma at the top clearly reads in large print "Purdue University." The proposed new PNW diploma at the bottom significantly transforms this to "Purdue University Northwest" while also subordinating the role of the Purdue University Trustees. (PNW Registrar's Archives)

tinue to receive a Purdue University degree as they had at the Hammond and Westville campuses prior to unification, on September 28 Chancellor Thomas Keon announced a new diploma that would replace the words "Purdue University" with "Purdue University Northwest." Vice Chancellor for Academic Affairs and Provost Ralph Mueller defended the move: "A clearly defined Purdue University Northwest diploma enhances the proud tradition of earning a degree from PNW's many quality, and nationally recognized, academic programs."[19] It was a rather disingenuous argument considering that PNW was then little more than two years old. A local newspaper reported that "PNW spokesman Doug Clark called the diploma change 'solely a design change,'" a statement that was demonstrably false since the new name very clearly implied something different from "Purdue University."[20]

There had been no consultation with students or faculty prior to the announcement. Reaction was immediate with a large student protest on Monday, October 1, followed by a petition drive that drew more than 18,000 signatures in just a few days, protests to University President Mitch Daniels, and direct appeals to the Purdue University Board of Trustees.[21] On October 7 the LaPorte County *Herald-Argus* reported that Republican State Senator Mike Bohacek was preparing to introduce a bill to require that diplomas from *all* "satellite campuses" in the state be identified by the name of the institution's main university. "Purdue University Northwest provides students the opportunity to earn a degree at a lower cost by living at home or commuting," Bohacek said. "The University promotes that students will earn a Purdue University degree. It is unfair for students who attend Purdue University Northwest to receive a degree distinguishing it as a satellite campus."[22] Presented with a veritable hurricane of outrage, when the Board of Trustees finally met on October 12, 2018, it soundly rejected the proposed change.[23] Nevertheless, the damage to PNW in the local communities remained.

The disastrous consequences of this string of ill-advised administrative decisions may have been lost on the PNW administration, but not on the students — or no doubt prospective students as well. In the January 22, 2019, issue of the *Pioneer*, student Amanda Lopez wrote:

> Westville class cancellations, travel requirements and growing frustration from faculty and students. Although at odds with the future-focused language of the university since unification, it's worth asking: How did we get here? The truth, it turns out, is in-line with the recurring themes present in PNW's short history: failed reciprocal communication, unilateral decisions and the placement of pride before recognition of fault.
>
> The recent Faculty Senate meetings have provided a micro-

cosm of such behavior, with faculty raising concerns about the imbalance between the two campuses and the future of the Westville campus in general, and administrators retorting that hostile perceptions from faculty and staff and a failure to adequately champion the Westville campus have resulted, at least partly, in its current state. During urgent situations such as this, blame is usual, but implicit in the blame is the question of accountability: Why didn't we see any of this coming?

In many ways, proper assessment by administrators before unification should have vetted the stability of two institutions that had vastly different enrollment demographics ... [and] pointed out the potential risk involved in combining two institutions with different strengths, weaknesses and enrollment figures, and the even higher risk of operating said two institutions with a one-size-fits-all approach.

The list of "should haves" is long and tedious and not all that useful now, however. In truth, many faculty, staff and students have moved on from unification-induced frustrations in the three and a half years since, focusing instead on improving the institution in whatever incremental way possible. What remains present in the attitudes of faculty, staff and students, though, is an unwavering mistrust toward PNW's administration. ... So, how did we get here?

Perhaps it was the combined failure of multiple administrations to assess the weaknesses of both campuses before unification. Perhaps a lack of value placed on faculty input resulted in the ignoring of many red flags. It's true: we cannot go back. But we could have started in a more well-educated and informed place.

The more urgent question still looms: where do we go from here?

According to our past mistakes, the emphasis should be on the collective "we." Mistakes provide learning opportunities, and PNW's long list may be what propels a robust and stable future – that is, if we choose to recognize and learn from them.[24]

The general effect of these administrative decisions, and the failure to keep the original promises made to students, was to reduce the student population on the Westville campus and to discourage new enrollments. What administrators apparently failed to consider was that students who live east or south of Westville have other options, such as attending Indiana University South Bend or even Indiana University

Northwest with shorter commutes and a wide variety of complete degree programs requiring no further travel. Similarly, the broken administrative promises seriously eroded faculty confidence in the PNW administration, leading to declining faulty morale and unintended promotion of an "us against them" paradigm. The net result was an unfortunately negative and harmful reputation for the new university in the surrounding communities.

While the above were major contributors to Westville's enrollment decline, other factors appeared to many students and community members to support the belief that the Westville campus would be closed, or at least reduced to a two-year institution. Some of these included the following:[25]

- There was no administrator "in charge" at Westville so that anyone wishing to use campus facilities or otherwise conduct business had to go to Hammond.

- Summer schedules were dramatically reduced at the Westville campus.

- At PNC, most majors projected course offering two to three years in advance to facilitate planning and students were able to enroll in classes up to three semesters in advance. With unification this ended so that it became more difficult for students to plan their academic programs. This lack of advanced scheduling and enrollment fed into the belief that Westville would be closing.

- In some majors, advisors actively began telling students they would have to travel to Hammond to complete their degrees at the same time administrators were denying that this was the case.

- Visits by admissions and recruiting staff to high schools in the Westville service area were reduced. Employees and community members with children in high school reported receiving no communications at all from the PNW admission staff.

- Active participation by PNW administrators in the Westville service area communities declined, and in some cases ceased.

- In combining the degree programs from the two campuses, the Hammond versions were almost invariably adopted which placed Westville students at a disadvantage in completing their degrees.

- Student activities at Westville were greatly curtailed and personnel reduced.

- Food service, technology support, and some other services at Westville declined exacerbating the inequitable support offered to students and faculty on the two campuses.

- Athletic teams practiced at Hammond and most games were played there, resulting in all but a handful of Westville athletes either transferring to Hammond or to another institution. This caused an estimated loss of nearly 100 students.

- Evening courses were reduced or eliminated, thereby excluding many working adults who could only attend evenings.

- Although promised more support for students and faculty as a result of unification, at Westville there was noticeably less.

All of these added incrementally to the negative perceptions among students and the public, reinforcing PNW's growing image problems, especially as they affected the Westville campus.

THE CONSEQUENCES OF UNIFICATION FOR PNC

When unification was announced the Purdue North Central campus in Westville was stable in both student and financial terms. Eliminating the large number of high school students obtaining college credit for their secondary school courses, the core enrollment of PNC had been relatively stable over the previous years. From fall 2011 through fall 2013, the core, degree-seeking PNC enrollment declined only slightly from 3,621 to 3,580 (1.1 percent) percent. During this same period core enrollment at Hammond was decreasing from 8,865 to 7,513 (15.3 percent).[26] Financially, prior to unification, although PNC went through a series of budget readjustments it was operating "in the black" while the Hammond campus was suffering serious operating deficits. Between fall 2008 and fall 2013 PNC added eleven full-time faculty, an increase of 9.2 percent while at Hammond there was a reduction in both adjunct and full-time faculty.[27]

Immediately following unification, enrollments at Westville plummeted due to a combination of the ill-advised administrative decisions described above and the refusal of administrators to adjust to meet the growing crisis. Similarly, Hammond enrollments continued their previous decline as seen in the following table.

TABLE 1: PURDUE NORTHWEST CORE ENROLLMENTS[28]

Fall	Westville		Hammond	
	Enrollment	% Change	Enrollment	% Change
2012*	3,573		8,186	
2013	3,580	+ 0.2	7,513	-8.2
2014**	3,287	- 8.2	7,386	- 1.7
2015***	3,221	- 2.0	6,998	- 5.3
2016	2,560	- 20.5	6,559	- 6.3
2017	2,222	- 13.2	6,449	- 1.7
2018	1,906	- 14.2	6,236	- 3.3
Change	- 1,167	- 46.7	- 1,950	- 23.8

* Pre-unification   ** Post-unification announcement
*** Unification begins

Although the administration attempted to blame these precipitate decreases on "faculty badmouthing unification" and an overall reduction in the availability of high school graduates in northwestern Indiana, these excuses were obviously false. For example, while the enrollment at the Westville campus fell by 46.7 percent, this was not reflected in its' major high school feeders as seen in the following table.

TABLE 2: GRADUATING CLASSES OF
MAJOR WESTVILLE FEEDER SCHOOLS[29]

High School	2013-14	2017-18
Chesterton	478	450
Knox	123	132
Kouts	72	70
LaPorte	354	388
Marquette	48	51
Michigan City	273	272

Morgan Twp	56	62
New Prairie	193	188
Portage	566	467
Valparaiso	469	433
Washington Twp	55	69
Westville	68	50
Total	2,755	2,632

As the data indicate, there was a reduction in the top twelve Westville feeder high schools of only 123 students or 4.5 percent. Thus, the suggestion that falling Westville enrollments were due to falling high school enrollments is obviously false.

Over the equivalent of nearly three generations, Purdue University North Central educated thousands of residents of north central Indiana and the surrounding areas. Businesses benefited from this education, while the community profited from the many social, cultural, and learning opportunities the campus and its faculty provided.

With unification, Purdue North Central as a distinct, identifiable entity ceased to exist. Given the precipitate decline in enrollment and reductions in support for the remaining students and faculty, at this writing it is questionable whether any recognizable semblance of the once-proud contributions of the Westville campus to the education of residents in north central Indiana will long survive in any form.

---

[1] PNW Unification Archive at https://www.pnw.edu/unification-archive/timeline-at-a-glance/.

[2] "Staff Summary Report to the Board of Trustees for Change of Control, Structure or Organization as Requested by Purdue University Calumet and Purdue University North Central" (January 26, 2016), 2., https://www.pnw.edu/unification-archive/wp-content/uploads/sites/71/2016/02/Staff-Summary-Report-Purdue-University-Calumet-and-Purdue-University-North-Central-012616.pdf.

[3] Christin Nance Lazerus, "Combined Purdue campuses 'changed amazingly,'" *Post-Tribune*, September 3, 2016.

[4] There was a wide variety of committees, the most critical being (1) Academic Structure (John Coffee, Hammond chair; James S. Pula, Westville chair), (2) Faculty Senate Constitution and Bylaws (Michael Dobberstein, Hammond chair; Heather Fielding, Westville chair), and (3) Promotion and Tenure (Janice Tazbir, Hammond chair; James S. Pula, Westville chair). Negotiations on the final draft of the Constitution and Bylaw was conducted by Harvey Abramowitz and Geoff Schultz at Hammond with Jeff Shires and Jonathan

Swarts representing Westville. PNC Faculty Senate Document 14-33 submitted April 13, 2015; Faculty Senate Ad Hoc Unification Task Force report, October 17, 2014; email, Jeff Shires to author, May 27, 2019.

[5] Letter, Barbara Gellman-Danley to Chancellors Thomas Keon and James Dworkin, March 3, 2016, announced Higher Learning Commissions approval for the merger (from https://www.pnw.edu/unification-archive/2016/03/04/hlc-action-letter-approving-purdue-northwest/).

[6] Steve Turner, PNW Vice Chancellor for Administration, PowerPoint presentation on "Historic Enrollment" presented to the Westville Study Committee in spring 2019 (hereafter cited as Turner, "Historic Enrollment"). The data does not include students receiving college credit for high school courses.

[7] Reports and discussions of the "Ad Hoc Committee for the Study of Westville" created by the PNW Faculty Senate (hereafter referred to as "Westville Study Committee").

[8] "Enrollment Summary Report – Fall 2018," Purdue University Northwest, Sept. 19, 2018, 1-7, PNW Archives; Turner, "Historic Enrollment."

[9] "Student and Parent FAQs Purdue University Northwest," brochure issued by PNW, October 2015; PNW Unification Archive, https://www.pnw.edu/unification-archive/faqs/.

[10] This statement, although it went unrecorded, was made by Provost Mueller in a PNW Faculty Senate meeting in the fall of 2016.

[11] Anne E. Gregory, "Welcome to the edTPA!," memorandum to students, January 12, 2018; Anne E. Gregory email to Alice Anderson, et al., November 7, 2017; draft resolution submitted by the Curriculum and Faculty Affairs Committees to the PNW Faculty Senate, March 1, 2018.

[12] "Students Against EdTPA: Accommodations Need to be Made," student online petition, spring 2018, https://www.change.org/p/purdue-northwest-school-of-education-and-counseling-students-against-edtpa-accommodations-need-to-be-made; student email contained in "Concerns Regarding an Unapproved Curriculum Requirement in the PNW School of Education and Counseling," report of the Faculty Affairs Committee to the Faculty Senate Executive Committee, spring 2018; draft resolution submitted by the Curriculum and Faculty Affairs Committees to the PNW Faculty Senate, March 1, 2018; various emails from students to administrators and trustees and responses from administrators (names of the students are withheld for their protection).

[13] "Students Against EdTPA; "Concerns Regarding an Unapproved Curriculum Requirement"; "Enrollment Summary Report – Fall 2018," Purdue University Northwest, Sept. 19, 2018, 1-7, PNW Archives; various emails from students to administrators and trustees and responses from administrators (names of the students are withheld for their protection).

[14] Editorial, Jacob Yothment, *Pioneer*, PNW student newspaper, April 18, 2017.

[15] Quoted in Amanda Biro, "Students, Faculty Provide Reflections, Concerns Following Unification," *Pioneer*, January 7, 2018.

[16] "Constitution of the Faculty of Purdue University Northwest," Sections III.B.2 and III.B.4.

[17] Email, Kathleen Tobin to James S. Pula, et al., November 19, 2017; email, Kathleen Tobin to James S. Pula, et al., November 20, 2017; email, Kathleen Tobin to James S. Pula, et al., December 11, 2017.

[18] Email, Kathleen Tobin to James S. Pula, et al., May 15, 2018; email, Kathleen Tobin to James S. Pula, et al., May 18, 2018; email, Michael J. Connolly to James S. Pula, et al., July 19, 2018; email, James S. Pula to Rita Brusca-Vega, September 13, 2018; email, James S. Pula to Rita Brusca-Vega, October 30, 2018.

[19] "Protests erupt after PNW announces name change on diploma," Chicago *Crusader*, October 8, 2018.

[20] "PNW diploma fight headed for Statehouse," LaPorte County *Herald-Argus*, October 7, 2018; "Protests erupt after PNW announces name change on diploma," Chicago *Crusader*, October 8, 2018.

[21] Ibid.

[22] "PNW diploma fight headed for Statehouse," LaPorte County *Herald-Argus*, October 7, 2018.

[23] Purdue University Board of Trustees Minutes, meeting of October 12, 2018, Purdue University Senate archives; PNW Faculty Senate minutes, October 12, 2018, PNW Archives.

[24] Amanda Lopez letter, *Pioneer*, January 22, 2019.

[25] The following bullet-points are taken from the reports and discussions of the "Ad Hoc Committee for the Study of Westville" created by the PNW Faculty Senate, and from its final report presented in Faculty Senate Document 18-12.

[26] Turner, "Historic Enrollment;" email from Gillian E. Leonard ro James S. Pula, March 5, 2019, with accompanying data.

[27] Board of Trustees, Purdue University, "Data Digest" for 2008-09 and 2013-14.

[28] Turner, "Historic Enrollment."

[29] Ibid.

TIMELINE

1862   Congress passes the Morrill Land-Grant Colleges Act

1865   Indiana voted to create an institution focusing "agriculture and the mechanic arts."

1874   Classes at Purdue begin

1887   Hatch Act helps establish experimental agricultural programs

1909   Establishment of Purdue agricultural extension program

1921   Purdue launches the engineering extension service

1935   Purdue begins classes in LaPorte County

1944   Servicemen's Readjustment Act passes Congress

1946   Purdue launches its extension program, which was the forerunner to the regional campuses

1948   Barker Mansion donated to Purdue

1953   Robert Schwarz hired as the Barker Center Director

1962   Ross-Ade Foundation buys 153 acres in Westville, Indiana

1967   Purdue North Central campus opens

1972   John W. Tucker becomes Chancellor of Purdue North Central

1973   Three new programs launched — the Child Care Center, Mini College, and the Bridge Programs

1975   The Library-Student-Faculty building opens

1979   William Fuller becomes Chancellor of PNC

1980   First baccalaureate degree offered at PNC (in Supervision)

1982   Dale Alspaugh becomes Interim Chancellor at PNC, permanent Chancellor in 1984.

1985   Classes begin at the Westville Correctional Center

1987   Industrial Engineering Technology Lab opens

1989   Chancellor Series begins

1995   Technology Building opens

1999   New baseball field opens

2000   James Dworkin becomes Chancellor at PNC

2000   Indiana Dunes Research Station opens

2003   Veterinary Emergency Center opens

2005   University Village apartments open

2006   Purdue University North Central gains academic autonomy

2006   Sanai Forum comes to PNC

2006   Purdue University North Central-Porter County opens in Valparaiso

2014   Merger of PNC with Purdue Calumet announced

2016   Dworkin Center opens

2016   PNC ceases to exist with the formal approval of Purdue University Northwest by the Higher Learning Commission accrediting organization

BIBLIOGRAPHY

Archival Material

"1945 Survey: Michigan City & LaPorte," PNW Archives.

"Ad Hoc Committee for the Study of Westville," documents and final report.

Allen, Virginia R., Barbara Ann Bardes, et al, "Report of a Visit to Purdue University-North Central for the Higher Learning Commission of the North Central Association of Colleges and Schools," April 25, 2001, Booklets Collection, PNW Archives.

Asteriadis, George T., and Debra A. Nielsen, eds., "Faculty Handbook for Academic Promotion and Tenure" (Westville, IN: PNC, 2005).

Beese, C. W. Correspondence, PNW Archives.

_____. "What is a Technical Institute?" (Dec. 17, 1946), PNW Archives.

Bergman, G. W. "M.E. University-Industry Cooperative Education Program" (1956), unpublished manuscript, PNW Archives.

"Chancellor's Advisory Board," August 10, 1979, Press Release Collection, PNW Archives.

"Chancellor's Resignation," December 9, 1981, Press Release Collection, PNW Archives.

"Child Care Center," Aug. 14, 1973, Press Release Collection, PNW Archives.

"Concerns Regarding an Unapproved Curriculum Requirement in the PNW School of Education and Counseling," report of the Faculty Affairs Committee to the PNW Faculty Senate Executive Committee, spring 2018.

Connelly, Carol. "PNC Increases Full-Time Student Numbers," Sept. 9, 2003, News Releases PNC Collection, Box 5, Sept. 2003, PNW Archives

_____. "Purdue North Central Sets Enrollment Record," Aug. 28, 2002, News Releases PNC Collection, Box 5, Aug. 2002, PNW Archives.

"Constitution of the Faculty of Purdue University Northwest," PNW Archives.

"Data Digest" Purdue University Board of Trustees Archives, West Lafayette, IN.

Dworkin, James. Interviewed by Joshua W. Koepke, Nov. 12, 2018,

West Lafayette, IN.

"Enrollment Summary Report," Fall 2016, Fall 2017 and Fall 2018, Purdue University Northwest, PNW Archives.

"Faculty Senate Ad Hoc Unification Task Force Report," Purdue North Central Faculty Senate, October 17, 2014, PNW Archives.

"Faculty Senate Document 14-01," PNC Faculty Senate, Sept. 2, 2014, https://faculty.pnw.edu/senate-north-central/wp-content/uploads/sit es/3/2014/09/14-01-Report-from-the-Faculty-Workshop-on-Issues-Surrounding-Unification.pdf.

Faculty Senate Document 14-33, Purdue North Central Faculty Senate, submitted April 13, 2015, PNW Archives.

Faculty Senate Minutes, PNC Faculty Senate, PNW Archives.

Faculty Senate Minutes, PNW Faculty Senate, PNW Archives.

"Farewell Dance," July 28, 1967, News Releases PNC, Box 1, Folder 10, NW Archives.

"Farewell to Barker," May 23, 1967, News Releases PNC, Box 1, Folder 10, PNW Archives.

Gellman-Danley, Barbara. Letter to Chancellors Thomas Keon and James Dworkin, March 3, 2016, from https://www.pnw.edu/ unification-archive/2016/03/04/hlc-action-letter-approving-purdue-northwest/.

"Geopolitics: Risk, Reward and Balance," https://www.pnw.edu/sinai-forum/geopolitics-risk-reward-and-balance/

Gregory, Anne E. "Welcome to the edTPA!," memorandum to students, January 12, 2018.

Hickox, Catherine. Correspondence, PNW Archives.

"Higher Learning Commission Self-Study" (Westville, IN: PNC, 2011).

Hovde, Frederick L. Correspondence, PNW Archives.

_____. "Purdue University," in "Purdue University North Central Institutional Self-Study, 1970" (Westville: Purdue North Central, 1970).

"Institutional Self-Study of Purdue University North Central Campus" (Westville, IN: Purdue North Central, 1981), PNW Archives.

"James Comey opens Purdue University Northwest Sinai Forum's 65th Season," April 16, 2018 (https://pnw.edu/news/james-comey-opens -purdue-university-northwest-sinai-forums-65th-season/

"James Dworkin," Purdue University Krannert School of Management, accessed November 29, 2018, https://krannert.purdue.edu/directory/bio.php?username=jdworkin.

Jones, Jeff. "Purdue North Central Enrollment Continues to Set Records," September 1, 2000, News Releases PNC Collection, Box 5, PNW Archives.

Kessell, A. R. Correspondence, PNW Archives.

Knapp, M. L. Correspondence, PNW Archives.

Lisarelli, Fredrick. "The First Ten Years of P.N.C. History" (1976), unpublished manuscript, PNW Archives.

Manny, Carter H. Correspondence, PNW Archives.

"Moving to New Campus," July 21, 1967, News Releases PNC, Box 1, Folder 10, NW Archives.

"New Bachelor of Liberal Studies Confirmed," September 9, 1981, Press Release Collection, PNW Archives.

"New Computer Technology Program," May 29, 1967, News Releases PNC, Box 1, Folder 10, PNW Archives.

News-clippings PNC, Box 1, Folders 3, 10-15, 17, 22-23, 25-27, 29, PNW Archives (contains clippings from various newspapers).

Nielsen, Debbie. "Unification Committee Meeting," July 10, 2015, Uploaded August 26, 2015 by Petersor, https://www.pnw.edu/unification-archive/2015/08/26/unification-committee-meeting-071015/.

"Organization for the Self-Study," in "Purdue University North Central Campus NCA Accreditation Data, 1970" (Westville, IN: Purdue University, 1970).

"Outlook of Purdue North Central," March 10, 1975, Press Release Collection, PNW Archives.

"Petition for Campus Academic Autonomy," August 16, 2005, Scrapbooks Collection, Box: "PNC Autonomy History '62-'06," PNW Archives.

PNC Faculty Senate Document 14-33 submitted April 13, 2015.

"PNC's First Mini College," October 3, 1973, Press Release Collection, PNW Archives.

PNW Unification Archive at https://www.pnw.edu/unification-archive/timeline-at-a-glance/.

"Prof. William R. Fuller Appointed as Interim Chancellor," March 27, 1979, Press Release Collection, PNW Archives.

Pula, James S. "Purdue North Central" (2007), unpublished manuscript courtesy of the author.

"Purdue North Central and the Communities," March 10, 1975, Press Release Collection, PNW Archives.

"Purdue North Central to Dedicate New Library-Student-Faculty Building," March 10, 1975, Press Release Collection, PNW Archives.

"Purdue University Approves Actions for Purdue North Central," May 28, 1975, Press Release Collection, PNW Archives.

Purdue University Board of Trustees minutes, Purdue University Libraries, Archives and Special Collections, Lafayette, Indiana.

"Purdue University Calumet University Senate Meeting Minutes," March 5, 2014, 4, http://faculty.pnw.edu/senate-calumet/wpcontent/uploads/sites/2/2014/03/FacultySenateMinutesMarch14.doc.

"Purdue University North Central Commencement," May 9, 2000, Commencement Collection, Box: Commencements 1990-2009, PNW Archives.

"Purdue University North Central Commencement," May 16, 2016, Archive and Special Collection, Box 1, PNW Archives.

"Purdue University North Central: Focused Visit Report 2003" (2003), Booklets Collection, PNW Archives.

"Purdue University North Central Institutional Self-Study, 1970" (Westville: Purdue North Central, 1970).

"Purdue University North Central Master Plan Report," November 2008, Sasaki Associates Inc., Strategic Plan Collection, Box 1, File 51, PNW Archives.

"Purdue University North Central Silver Anniversary" (1992), unpublished manuscript, PNW Archives.

"Purdue University Northwest Interactive Fact Book," Purdue University Northwest, 2018, https://www.pnw.edu/planning-institutional-effectiveness/factbook/.

Purdue University Northwest Unification Archive at https://www.pnw.edu/unification-archive/timeline-at-a-glance/.

"Purdue University Regional Campus Administration Annual Report 1969-70" (West Lafayette, IN: Purdue University, 1970), Section 5.

"Purdue University Regional Campus Administration Annual Report 1970-1971" (West Lafayette: Purdue University, 1971), Section 5.

"Purdue's Hovde Compares Area Campus to 'Original,'" April 20, 1967, News Releases PNC, Box 1, Folder 10, PNW Archives.

"Report of Publicity Activities, July-September 1947," Purdue University Technical Extension Division, PNW Archives.

Ringel, Robert L. Email to James Dworkin, Dec. 18, 2000, Scrapbooks Collection, Box: "PNC Autonomy History '62-'06," PNW Archives.

Roberts, Cynthia. Interviewed by Joshua W. Koepke, Nov. 2, 2018, Valparaiso, IN.

Salle, L. James, letter to Deborah Kohler, April 28, 2016, copy in the possession of Joshua Koepke.

Schwarz, Robert. "First Ten Years of P.N.C. History" (1964), unpublished manuscript in the PNW Archives.

"Section II—Analysis of Self-Study Reports," in "Regional Campus Summary Report: North Central Self-Study July 1, 1971" (West Lafayette, IN: Purdue University, 1971).

Short, Harry C. Correspondence, PNW Archives.

"Space Utilization Committee Report and Recommendations," May 1, 2006, Booklets Collection, PNW Archives.

"Staff Summary Report to the Board of Trustees for Change of Control, Structure or Organization as Requested by Purdue University Calumet and Purdue University North Central" (January 26, 2016), https://www.pnw.edu/unification-archive/wp-content/uploads/sites/71/2016/02/Staff-Summary-Report-Purdue-University-Calumet-and-Purdue-University-North-Central-012616.pdf.

"Student and Parent FAQs Purdue University Northwest," brochure issued by PNW, October 2015, PNW Unification Archive, https://www.pnw.edu/unification-archive/faqs/.

"Students Against EdTPA: Accommodations Need to be Made," student online petition, spring 2018.

Turner, Steve. "Historic Enrollment" PowerPoint presentation to the PNW Senate's Westville Study Committee, spring 2019.

"Two Bachelor Degrees Approved," May 9, 1980, Press Release Collection, PNW Archives.

Waterhouse, Ralph. Correspondence, PNW Archives.

Westville Study Committee reports, committee documents.

Published Sources

"A Believer in Education," *Times*, June 28, 1999.

Alspaugh, Dale. "Indiana Facing 'Brain Drain' Crisis," *Michigan City News-Dispatch*, Oct. 1, 1983.

_____. "It's Not Too Late to Continue Your Education," *Michigan City News-Dispatch*, Jan. 13, 1984.

_____. "Up to You," *Westville Indicator*, Nov. 4, 1982.

"Alspaugh Proud of Improvements in Quality, Service: Retired Administrator saw North Central through Rapid Growth," *Inside Purdue*, January 25, 2000.

"Barker Homestead Given to Purdue University for Use as Class Center," *The News Dispatch*, Jan. 22, 1948.

Bartholomew, Charles M. "New Activity Center Awaits PNC Students," *Post Tribune*, July 11, 2001.

Biro, Amanda, "Students, Faculty Provide Reflections, Concerns Following Unification," *Pioneer* (PNW student newspaper), January 7, 2018.

Bishop, Amanda. "Groundbreaking for PNC Veterinary Center," *La Porte County Herald-Argus*, June, 2002.

_____. "PNC's Enrollment Rises Slightly Over Last Year," *La Porte County Herald Argus*, Sept. 10, 2001.

_____. "Terrific Deal for Selected MC Students," *La Porte County Herald-Argus*, Jan. 28, 2004.

_____. "When Your Dog Turns Blue and it's After Hours," *La Porte County Herald-Argus*, March 6, 2003.

Bound, John and Sarah Turner, "Going to War and Going to College: Did World War II and the G.I. Bill Increase Educational Attainment for Returning Veterans?" *Journal of Labor Economics*, Vol. 20, no. 4 (Oct. 2002).

"Business Classes Offered," *Michigan City News-Dispatch*, August 5, 2001.

Carlson, Carole. "Enrollment Up: Number of Students Increasing despite Higher Tuition," *Post Tribune*, Sept. 30, 2003.

_____. "PNC Discloses Housing Plans: Proposed Development Would Have 150 Apartments," *Post Tribune*, Sept. 23, 2003.

_____. "PUNC, Dogs Break Ground," *Post Tribune*, Dec. 8, 2001.

_____. "Purdue North Central Plans $30 Million Housing Project," *Chesterton Tribune*, Sept. 23, 2003.

_____. "Students as Residents: Purdue University North Central

Building Student-Apartment Complex," *Post Tribune*, Oct. 6, 2004.

_____. "Valparaiso University Records Largest Hike Among Area Colleges," *Post Tribune*, Sept. 29, 2004.

Castle, Courtney, and Julia Johnson, "For After-Hours Veterinary Care, Go to Emergency Clinic," *NWI Times*, June 8, 2003.

Chambers, Richard. "Burgwald Seeking Re-Election to School Board," *Michigan City News-Dispatch*, Aug. 17, 2014.

"Childhood Education Program Recognized," *NWI Times*, March 27, 2014.

Clarke, Olivia. "Governor Expands Community College System," *NWI Times*, Oct. 6, 2004.

"Computers in Classes, Offices, Club at PNC," *Westville Indicator*, Nov. 25, 1982.

"Dean Selection Group Meets," *Vidette-Messenger* (Valparaiso, IN), December 8, 1971.

Domschke, Azure. "New PNC Chancellor Wants New Buildings," *NWI Times*, Jan. 14, 2000.

_____. "Technology Building Renovations Complete: New Labs, Classrooms, Offices will be Open for Full Semester," *NWI Times*, June 5, 2000.

_____. "Valparaiso Academic Center will Offer Undergraduate Courses, Business Training," *Times*, Sept. 12, 2000.

Dworkin, James. James B. Dworkin, "Exciting Change Coming to PNC," *Michigan City News Dispatch*, Nov. 15, 2001.

_____. "Guest Commentary: PNC Career Always About Student Access, Success," *NWI Times*, (Munster, IN), June 26, 2016.

Fritz, Mat. "Daniels Addresses Issues at PNC," *Michigan City News Dispatch*, April 27, 2012.

Haverstick, Amanda. "City Savings Bank of Michigan City has Joined the College Bound Program with a Five-Year Financial Commitment for $25,000," *Michigan City News-Dispatch*, Feb. 18, 2005.

Holmes, Elizabeth. "Ivy Tech, PNC Sign Partnership Agreement," *NWI Times*, March 30, 2006.

"IUN Sees Enrollment Increase," *Post-Tribune*, Sept. 12, 2009.

LaFrance, Catherine. "PNC Partners with Sinai," *La Porte County Herald-Argus*, August, 8, 2006.

Lazerus, Christin Nance. "Combined Purdue Campuses 'changed amazingly,'" *Post-Tribune*, September 3, 2016.

Lopez, Amanda. Letter, *Pioneer* (PNW student newspaper), January 22, 2019.

Lords, Erik. "With a New Community-College System, Indiana Hopes for More Skilled Workers," *Chronicle of Higher Education*, August 18, 2000.

Loughlin, Sue. "IDOC Changing Inmate Education: Along with Funding Degrees to Focus on Employment," *Tribune-Star,* Press Clippings Collection, File: May 2011, PNW Archives.

Maddux, Stan. "Authorities: Underage Drinking Party Busted: Eight Cited for Alcohol, and Officers Pour Drinks Down the Kitchen Sink," *Times*, April 6, 2011.

_____. "Bus Service to PNC Approved," *NWI Times*, Oct. 17, 2014.

_____. "Bus Service Stays Optimistic," *NWI Times*, Feb. 19, 2015.

_____. "Cops Raid Two Parties near PNC, Arrest 17," *Post-Tribune*, Sept. 23, 2006.

_____. "Funds Freed for PNC Activities Site: Facility Offering Home for Athletic Teams and Recreation," *Times*, May 2, 2013.

_____. "More's the Word for New Purdue North Central Boss," *Post-Tribune,* (Chicago, IL), Jan. 14, 2000.

_____. "Purdue Campus to Offer Bachelor's in Nursing," *South Bend Tribune,* (South Bend, IN), Feb. 22, 2004.

_____. "Underage Party-Goers End Night with Arrests," *Post Tribune*, Nov. 28, 2006.

_____. "Westville Area Man Falls From Second-Floor Balcony during Party," *Times*, Sept. 16, 2013.

"Mayor Names Jeff Jones to Board," The *Michigan City News-Dispatch* (Michigan City, IN), Oct. 19, 2002.

McArdle, Michael. "Purdue Field Station Finds Home Inside Dunes," *Post Tribune*, July 12, 2000.

McCollum, Carmen. "Schools Focused on College Completion: Commission Report Details Grad Rates," *NWI Times*, Feb. 19, 2014, A5.

"Michigan City Area Chamber of Commerce Announces 2014 Board

Members and Officers," *NWI Times* (Munster, IN), Jan. 27, 2014.

Miller, Jason. "Party Leads to Arrests," *Michigan City News Dispatch*, Nov. 10, 2007.

"Minors Cited at PNC Apartments," *La Porte County Herald Argus*, Nov. 17, 2006.

"New Dean Named at PNC," *News-Dispatch*, June 26, 1972.

Nicholas, John. "PNC Chancellor to Stay-for a While," *South Bend Tribune*, June, 29, 1999.

"19 Arrested at Parties near PNC," *La Porte County Herald Argus*, Sept. 22, 2006.

"North Central Veterinary Center to Open 24/7 on March 28," *Westville Indicator*, March 24, 2011.

O'Brien, Jessica. "New PNW Complex Opens," *La Porte County Herald-Argus*, May 25, 2016.

Olson, Keith W. "The G.I. Bill and Higher Education: Success and Surprise," *American Quarterly*, Vol. 25, no. 5 (Dec. 1973).

Petreikis, Dan. "Purdue University North Central Holds Forty-Eight Commencement Ceremony in New Campus Expansion," *Valpolife.com*, May 17, 2016.

"Plans for Developing PNC are Announced," *News-Dispatch*, May 24, 1972.

"PNC Approved to Change 'Divisions' to 'Colleges,'" *NWI Times*, June 10, 2006.

"PNC Baseball Players Fight Over Pizza," *La Porte County Herald Argus*, May 8, 2006.

"PNC Bidding 2nd Building Announced," *LaPorte Herald-Argus*, May 12, 1972.

"PNC Chancellor Alspaugh to Retire," *LaPorte Harold-Argus*, March 25, 1999.

"PNC Chancellor Awarded," *Beacher*, Oct. 23, 2014.

"PNC College Bound Partnership," *Beacher* (Michigan City, IN), March 30, 2006.

"PNC Curriculum Revisions Help Students Earn Degrees," *La Porte County Herald-Argus*, May 17, 2012.

"PNC Education Looks at Future Programs," *LaPorte Herald-Argus*, January 16, 1973.

"PNC Enrollment at All-Time High," *Michigan City News Dispatch*, Sept. 4, 2007.

"PNC Establishes Indiana Dunes Research Station," *Michigan City News Dispatch*, July 13, 2000.

"PNC Has Slight Decrease in Enrollment Numbers," *Michigan City News Dispatch*, Sept. 25, 2015.

"PNC Increases Student Numbers, Sets Credit Hours Record," *The Voice*, Aug. 20, 2005.

"PNC Offering Bachelor's in Human Resources," *NWI Times*, Feb. 23, 2009.

"PNC Offers Tuition Discount Program," *La Porte County Herald Argus*, March 13, 2014.

"PNC Officials Elated Over Afro Week Events," *LaPorte Herald-Argus* (La Porte, IN), February 21, 1972.

"PNC Paper Seeks 'Relevance,'" *News-Dispatch* (Michigan City, IN), March 11, 1972.

"PNC Professor, Students Work on Computerized Production Line," *LaPorte Herald-Argus*, Feb. 27, 1984.

"PNC Sets Enrollment and Credit Hour Records," *Westville Indicator*, Sept. 18, 2008.

"PNC Sets Enrollment and Credit Hour Records," *Westville Indicator*, Sept. 19, 2013.

"PNC Sets Enrollment, Credit Hour Records," *La Porte County Herald Argus*, Sept. 13, 2011.

"PNC Sets Enrollment Record," *Beacher*, 36, Sept. 17, 2009.

"PNC Sets Enrollment Record," *La Porte County Herald Argus*, Aug. 30, 2012.

"PNC Sets Enrollment Records," *Michigan City News Dispatch*, Sept. 2, 2010.

"PNC Sets Record for Enrollment," *La Porte County Herald Argus*, Sept. 6, 2006.

"PNC Students Arrested at Party," *Michigan City News Dispatch*, Jan. 21, 2009.

"PNC to Celebrate Groundbreaking on October 16," *Westville Indicator*, October 2, 2014.

"PNC to Observe Afro-American History Week," *Vidette-Messenger*, February 3, 1972.

"PNC to Offer New Engineering Degree," *Michigan City News-*

Dispatch, Nov. 13, 2007.

"PNC to Offer 2 New Degree Programs," *Michigan City News-Dispatch*, May 15, 2012.

"PNC Offers Tuition Discount Programs," *NWI Times*, June 29, 2015, A7.

"PNC Tuition Discount Program Tallies $100,000 in Student Savings," *Westville Indicator*, August 7, 2014.

"PNW Diploma Fight Headed for Statehouse," La Porte County *Herald-Argus*, October 7, 2018.

"Protests Erupt After PNW Announces Name Change on Diploma," Chicago *Crusader*, October 8, 2018.

"Purdue North Central Sets Enrollment Record," *La Porte County Herald Argus*, Sept.12, 2014.

Przybyla, Daniel. "Joined Together: A Better Future Targeted by New Alliance," *La Porte County Herald Argus*, Feb. 21, 2004.

"Record Enrollment Puts PNC Campus at Top Tier," *Post Tribune*, Sept. 21, 2006.

Rich, Robert. "The Great Recession," *Federal Reserve History*, Nov. 22, 2013.

Richards, Rick A. "PNC Receives 'Full Academic Autonomy,'" *Michigan City News-Dispatch*, Feb. 8, 2006.

Rogers, Sarah *Barker Mansion: Heritage with a Future* (Berrien Center, MI: Penrod/Hiawatha, 2000).

Ross, Doug. "Comey Defends Decision in 2016 Clinton Announcement at Sinai Forum in Michigan City," *NWI Times*, Sept. 9, 2018.

Russell, Joyce. "Portage Inks PNC Lease: University Will Use Two Classrooms in University Center," *NWI Times*, Nov. 30, 2012.

Sederberg, Deborah. "Apartments Across from PNC Filling Up," *Michigan City News Dispatch*, Sept. 12, 2005.

_____. "Organizations Donate to College Bound Fund," *Michigan City News-Dispatch*, June 5, 2004.

_____. "PNC Adds Social Work Degree," *Starke County Leader* (Knox, IN), Oct. 29, 2009.

_____. "PNC Building was a Priority for Bowser," *Michigan City News Dispatch*, March 6, 2007.

_____. "PNC Project Benefits Students," *Michigan City News Dispatch*, July 11, 2001.

_____. "PNC to Offer New Degrees," *Michigan City News-Dispatch*, May 19, 2001.

"Seven Arrested Playing 'Beer Pong,'" *La Porte County Herald-Argus*, August 25, 2006.

"Shabby Treatment by PNC Administration is Charged," *News-Dispatch*, April 29, 1972.

Siddiqi, Asif A. "Competing Technologies, National(ist) Narratives, and Universal Claims: Toward a Global History of Space Exploration," *Technology and Culture*, Vol. 51, no. 2 (Apr. 2010).

"State Revenue Shortfall Likely to Affect PNC," *Michigan City News-Dispatch*, Aug. 5, 1982.

"Technical Institute Training Offered at LaPorte and Michigan City," *Starke County Democrat*, Aug. 6, 1947.

"The State's Highest Honor," *Michigan City News-Dispatch*, May 7, 1999.

"Transit Triangle Offers Convenient Travel," *Westville Indicator*, July 9, 2015.

Trusty, Lance. *Purdue University Calumet: The First Fifty Years* (Hammond, IN: Purdue University Calumet, 1996).

"United Way is Set to Recognize PNC," *Times*, (Munster, IN), Feb. 23, 2009.

"Valpo's PUNC Site Gets a Name Change," *Post Tribune*, Feb. 25, 2006.

"Wells Fargo Donation to Aid Qualifying Students," *Michigan City News Dispatch*, Oct. 26, 2006.

Werner, Deborah. "PNC Opens New Student Facility in Library," *NWI Times*, July 2001.

Williams, Brian. "Ivy Tech Shows Off New Digs," *NWI Times*, May 26, 2006.

_____. "Purdue Board Oks $1.1B for its Schools: Trustees Meet at PNC to Discuss Budget Woes," *NWI Times*, April 10, 2010.

Wolf, James D., Jr., "PNC Breaks Ground on new Student Complex," *Post Tribune*, October 17, 2014.

_____. "Purdue Campus in Valpo Gets Old Ivy Tech Parking," *Post Tribune*, Jan. 23, 2009.

"Woodward Kicks off Forum Season," *Michigan City News-Dispatch*, August 28, 2006.

Yothment, Jacob. Editorial, *Pioneer* (PNW student newspaper), April 18, 2017.

INDEX

Joseph Coates is a native of Hammond, Indiana, with a B.G.S. from Indiana University Northwest, and an M.S.L.S. from Clarion University of Pennsylvania. He has been the Archivist of Calumet College of St Joseph in Whiting, Indiana and is currently the University Archivist at Purdue University Northwest. Joe is a Navy veteran whose interests include the history of the Calumet Region, digital humanities, management of small repositories, and experiential learning. He lives in Val-

paraiso, Indiana with his wife Annette, and his two daughters, Abigail and Rebecca.

James S. Pula received his B.A. from the State University of New York at Albany, an M. Ed. from the University of Maryland, and M.A. and Ph.D. degrees from Purdue University. A specialist in immigration studies and nineteenth century American history, he is the author or editor of more than twenty books, and has received awards for his research from the Milwaukee Country Historical Society, the U.S. Army Historical Foundation, the Polish Institute of Arts & Sciences, Polonica Technica, the Polish American Historical Association, and the Republic of Poland.

Printed in the USA
CPSIA information can be obtained
at www.ICGtesting.com
LVHW052054181223
766832LV00010B/176